WALL
STREET
JOURNAL
BOOKS

NETWORTH

Successful Investing in the Companies*
That Will Prevail through Internet Booms and Busts

*(They're Not Always the Ones You Expect)

STEPHEN E. FRANK

A WALL STREET JOURNAL BOOK
Published by Simon & Schuster
NEW YORK   LONDON   TORONTO   SYDNEY   SINGAPORE

WALL
STREET
JOURNAL
BOOKS

A WALL STREET JOURNAL BOOK
Published by Simon & Schuster, Inc.
1230 Avenue of the Americas
New York, NY 10020

10   9   8   7   6   5   4   3   2   1

Library of Congress Cataloging-in-Publication Data
Frank, Stephen E.
   Network: successful investing in the companies
that will prevail through Internet booms and busts
(they're not always the ones you expect) / Stephen
E. Frank.
      p.   cm.
   Includes index.
   1. Internet industry—Finance.   2. Investment
analysis.   I. Title.
HD9696.8.A2 F73 2001
332.63'22—dc21   2001020327
ISBN 0-7432-1093-X

for Mom, Dad, and Omi

Contents

NETWORTH

Helping You Help Yourself

Throughout most of the late 1990s, you didn't need to be an investment genius to make money on Internet stocks. All you needed to do was to pick something with a dot com in its name, and you were pretty much guaranteed a winner. For investors who sat on the sidelines—afraid to get involved in a market that seemed unsustainable but envying others who did—it was a painful time.

Then came the spring of 2000. As a stock-crushing technology bear market took hold in the months that followed, those who remained invested in the dot-com revolution suffered a rout. Indeed, it seemed, the only way to make money on Net stocks at that point was to bet on their decline. Many savvy investors did just that. Others who had watched, stupefied, as the Internet bubble inflated, now reveled in its implosion.

Here's the bad news: the days of easy money are over.

Here's the good news: the market's shakeout performed much of the dirty work that was needed to separate the Internet's long-term survivors from the fly-by-nights. Some work remains to be done. But the demise of so many dot coms means—a bit counterintuitively—that for everyone who sat out the market's gravity-defying rise, the time to get involved may finally have arrived.

This book is for those investors.

It aims to cut through the overstatement and the hype that accompany so much of what is said about the Internet and to help you better understand *how* the medium works, *who* stands to benefit from it and be harmed by it, and *why* it makes sense for investors, however cautiously, to weave Internet-related investments through their investment portfolios. *Networth* isn't for day traders, nor does it advocate the dangerous style of hyperkinetic buying and selling of stocks these gamblers have introduced to the marketplace. The book also doesn't recommend specific securities, in part because those types of recommendations could quickly become obsolete and in part because different stocks make sense for different investors. But no matter what your investment style may be, *Networth* will help you know what to look for. It will give you a better grasp of key concepts and major players in Internet investing so that you can make smarter, better-informed investment decisions on your own.

The book begins with an introduction to the ABCs of Internet investing, including a brief overview of the history and evolution of the Net and a framework for understanding the sector's component parts. Chapter Two offers an examination of a single company, AOL Time Warner, that stands as a paradigm of the new kind of corporation the Internet makes possible. Precisely because it isn't a "pure-play" dot com—because it has real-world assets and infrastructure and actually derives the bulk of its revenues from off-line activities—AOL Time Warner is a perfect example of the company of the future. It is a company whose heritage straddles the on-line and off-line worlds and whose future aims to blend the best of both. It is, in short, *infused* by the Net, inextricably bound to the Net, but not exclusive to the Net. And in that way, it resembles what the vast majority of successful companies will look like one day—with one foot firmly planted on-line and one firmly planted off-line. Chapter Three takes a close look at dot-com companies that aim their products or services at consumers: portals, news sites, retailers, and auction sites. It examines how these models work and how they're expected to evolve. The chapter also includes a few "company snapshots" of major players in the field. These snapshots—which are included in several later chapters as well—aren't designed to be comprehensive investment profiles, nor should they be used, on their own, to make investment decisions. Instead, they are jumping-off points—glimpses of how a handful of interesting companies and mutual funds do business and how they're performing at a particular moment in time. Chapter Four delves into business between businesses on the Net—the fastest-growing segment of on-line commerce—with an emphasis on Internet consultants, Internet advertising networks, and the specialized portals that have sprung up to facilitate business-to-business, or "B2B," transactions. Chapter Five lays out the physical world of the "Internet backbone"—from servers, switches, and routers to the software that helps power Web sites. Chapter Six looks at Internet proxy investments—ways of betting on the growth of the Net without actually investing in Internet companies—from distribution and fulfillment companies to chip makers to telecom providers. Chapter Seven addresses the stock market's love-hate relationship with Net stocks and discusses how to value Internet companies and how to include Internet-related investments in a broader investment portfolio. Chapter Eight explores the world of mutual funds and venture capital. While most venture capital firms don't allow average investors to participate, some do. This chapter identifies some of the leading "Internet incubators" and examines the variety of mutual funds that emphasize Internet investments. Finally, Chapter Nine speculates on the post-PC era, when everything from our wristwatches to our microwave ovens will be Internet-ready and when investors will finally stop drawing distinctions between Internet companies and non-Internet companies.

With Net stocks soaring one day and crashing the next, you're bound to be wondering: Is it too late? Have I missed the boat? (And should I be thanking my lucky stars I did?) The answer is no, on all three counts. But that doesn't mean you should dawdle.

The Internet is here to stay, though that's not true of every company that tries to take advantage of it. And the Internet *will* change everything—or at least a lot of things. But it's still early in the ball game. The day will come, as this book argues, when the world will not be divided between dot coms and non–dot coms; every company will be, to one degree or another, an Internet company. For you as an investor, it's important to know what that means and how to position your own portfolio to profit from the transition.

CHAPTER ONE

It's Not Too Late

*The Revolution
You Can't Afford to Miss*

THERE ARE LOTS of bad reasons to invest in the Internet. Among them is the notion that Internet investing is a road to a quick buck. Internet stocks, according to this logic, may or may not be around forever, but it doesn't matter. Their volatile trading patterns mean that the nimble investor can make a fast profit regardless of the long-term outlook. The fancy name for this is momentum investing: the practice of buying a stock for no other reason than that it's moving higher. But don't be fooled; investing has little to do with it. In its most extreme form—day trading—momentum investing involves jumping in and out of stocks over the course of a few hours, barely pausing to find out their names, in the hope of making a lot of money off of moves of just a few points. Momentum investing gained a broad following during the tech-stock craze of 1999 but became a lot less popular during the tech-stock sell-off of 2000.

This book has an altogether different approach. It's premised on the notion that the Internet is here to stay but the spectacularly volatile way Internet stocks have traded in recent years isn't. Already, the once-frenzied rush to invest in anything remotely connected to the Net has ended as a growing number of formerly high-flying dot coms have gone bust. Yet more than a few companies continue to sport billion-dollar market values despite having no profits, meager sales, and heavy competition. Couple that with fickle investors who repeatedly shift from one subsector and business model to another, and investing in Internet stocks has become the most exciting—and terrifying—investment theme in years. Millions of investors have thrown billions of dollars at Net stocks in hopes of reaping huge rewards. Some have. Others have lost their shirts.

If all that turmoil has you sitting on the sidelines of Internet investing, don't worry, you have plenty of company. Yet there's no need to be paralyzed. This book is aimed at investors who know the Internet is changing the world but haven't determined how to use that knowledge in their investment portfolios. It has three underlying principles:

1. The Internet is for real (but that isn't true of every Internet company).

2. It isn't too late to become an Internet investor.

3. The "secrets" of investing in the Internet are the same secrets of making any investment: do your homework, know what you're buying, invest for the long haul, and don't buy stocks that will keep you awake at night.

Here's the bad news: Among the hundreds of Internet companies that have gone public in recent years, most will flame out. Two of the most prominent Internet stock analysts, Morgan Stanley's Mary Meeker and Merrill Lynch's Henry Blodget, predict that as many as three quarters of the dot coms that have gone public within the last couple of years will cease to exist within the next couple. Their revenues and profits won't materialize, their stocks will plummet, and they'll either wither slowly on the vine, go out of business, or be sold. It's already happening. Remember ToySmart, Living.com, and Boo.com? Jeff Bezos, the thirtysomething founder and chairman of Amazon.com—the largest of the Web-only retailers—cheerfully jokes that his firm is "famous for losing money," warning prospective investors that Amazon "is not yet a lasting company" and may never become one. "The track record of innovators is not good," Mr. Bezos frequently intones.

But that doesn't mean the Internet itself—or every Internet company—will suffer a sorry fate. Quite the opposite. A few dot coms that today seem like the most speculative of bets will almost certainly rank one day among the greatest success stories in the history of business. Investors fortunate enough to get in early on these future giants will be richly rewarded. Many other companies, meanwhile, will become more modest successes, even if they don't live up to the hype of their early days. The tough part of all this, it goes without saying, is sorting the long-term winners from the losers. That's where this book is designed to help.

The Living Dead

Already, the proverbial separation of the wheat from the chaff is well under way. Consider theglobe.com, a business founded by two twenty-five-year-old Cornell graduates as an on-line meeting place for people with similar interests. One of the earliest examples of such "community"-oriented Web sites, theglobe.com went public in late 1998 in one of the most spectacular initial public stock offerings in history. Its stock, priced at $9 a share, opened at $90 before settling back. But theglobe.com never came close to regaining those first-day highs, and by late 1999—barely one year after its IPO—the company had issued its first formal warning that its quarterly results wouldn't meet expectations. In early 2000, the two founders resigned as co–chief executives. And although, as of early 2001, theglobe.com remained in business, it continued to lose money and its stock was clinging to life at pennies a share.

Another example: Value America, one of the early darlings of Internet commerce, was founded on the intuitively appealing idea that the Web eliminates the need for retailers to carry inventory and, to the contrary, means they can offer customers a limitless selection of products. With financial backing from blue-chip names such as FedEx and Microsoft cofounder Paul Allen, Value America launched a flashy coast-to-coast advertising campaign, tantalizing consumers with rock-bottom prices for everything from toasters to toothpaste. But Value America's promise also faded quickly. The hugely expensive marketing effort failed to draw many customers;

those who came were disappointed with uneven service (a symptom of the same inventoryless model that made the company so attractive to investors); and the razor-thin profit margins hadn't a prayer of stanching the firm's hemorrhage of capital. By early 2000, Value America had announced drastic plans to scale back its advertising, curtail its product offerings, refocus its sales efforts, and fire half of its staff. A few months later, it had filed for Chapter 11 bankruptcy protection, hoping to reorganize and reemerge with a new business strategy.

A third example: TheStreet.com, a Web site devoted to financial news and content, was created by a high-profile money manager (James Cramer of the Cramer, Berkowitz hedge fund) and a high-profile publisher (Martin Peretz of *The New Republic*), staffed by veterans of some of the nation's most respected news organizations, and backed by such established names as *The New York Times*. But after a promising start, TheStreet.com also faltered. Despite high-quality content, it failed to attract enough paying subscribers, resorting first to free promotional giveaways to drive subscriptions and ultimately scrapping the paid-subscription model almost entirely. A management shake-up and a public pledge by Mr. Cramer to take stock options in lieu of a salary failed to do much for the company's stock, which following an early pop has remained a lackluster performer. In early 2000, TheStreet.com confirmed that it had hired an investment bank to "explore alternatives," and later that year the company laid off part of its staff and closed its European operations.

Theglobe.com, Value America, and TheStreet.com are all examples of companies that, although unprofitable as businesses and unsuccessful as investments, refuse to die. They linger on—the living dead of the new economy—clinging to the hope that they'll either be bought or their luck will improve before they run out of money. Ironically, these three companies are among the fortunate ones. They arrived on the scene early enough and garnered enough publicity that they were able to capture investors' imaginations, raising so much money through both private and public rounds of financing that they are able, for now, to remain in operation, though each of them continues to bleed red ink. In the meantime, hundreds of other, lesser-known firms in similar circumstances have been forced to merge, sell their operations at bargain-basement prices, or shut down. They are names destined to be forgotten amid one of the greatest technological revolutions—and speculative bubbles—the world has known.

The New Elite

But for all these failures, a few companies have already achieved stunning successes unimaginable just a few years ago. In 1999, eBay—the on-line auctioneer that allows millions of ordinary people to conduct business with one another in a global flea market—purchased the century-old Butterfield and Butterfield auction house, the first significant example of an Internet-age company overtaking, and subsuming, an old-world rival. A few months later, Internet service provider America Online—a fifteen-year-old company written off by some as doomed just a couple of years earlier—acquired Time Warner, the world's largest media conglomerate and owner of some of the most prestigious brands in television and print. And then there's Yahoo!, the giant among so-called Internet portal sites. A company with no real-world assets to speak of, founded by two graduate students on leave from Stanford University, Yahoo! was added to the Standard & Poor's 500 stock index in late 1999, just six years after its founding. Though it has repeatedly disclaimed any interest in doing so, Yahoo! has at times been cited as a potential merger partner for venerable behemoths in the traditional media ranging from News Corporation to the Walt Disney Company. In contrast to the living dead, these three firms are examples of the economy's new elite—companies with hugely promising business models that dominate their competition to an extent rarely seen in the annals of American business.

The Big Picture

More broadly, the Internet as a repository of content, a medium of communications, and a mode of commerce will become ever more entrenched in our daily lives. Worldwide, the number of people using the Net is expected to top half a *billion* in 2004, up from about half that level in 2000 and from less than 40 *million* as recently as 1996, according to International Data Corporation. And some studies suggest that those numbers are conservative, because they assume that Internet users will rely only on personal computers or Internet-ready TV sets and don't take into account newer, cheaper, and more ubiquitous Internet access devices such as cellular phones and personal digital assistants. Already, the Web has utterly reshaped the way many of us shop, study, and conduct business. Don't feel like heading in to the office anymore? In 1999, according to Forrester Research, nearly a third of North American households were linked to the Net with the express purpose of allowing someone to work from home. Don't feel like doing the grocery shopping? In 1999, $513 million worth of groceries was sold on-line, up from $90 million just three years earlier. And Forrester expects that number to hit nearly $17 *billion* by 2004. So complete and so rapid has this transformation been that more than a few commentators have worried that we're becoming a nation of hermits, content to while away our lives in the isolation of our own homes, interacting with the outside world solely via mouse, keyboard, and telephone. "The more hours people use the Internet, the less time they spend with real human beings," Stanford University political scientist Norman Nie told *The New York Times.* "When you spend your time on the Internet, you don't hear a human voice and you never get a hug." A study by Mr. Nie found that of those Americans who spend more than five hours per week on-line, 13 percent spend less time with family and friends and 8 percent attend fewer social events. Perhaps not surprisingly, a 1999 Roper Starch poll commissioned by America Online showed that 66 percent of Americans surveyed would prefer an Internet connection to a telephone (23%) or a television set (8%) if stranded on a desert island.

Even as it reshapes our personal habits, the Internet's unprecedented ability to heighten business efficiency—by eliminating the need for costly physical infrastructure, improving awareness of prices, and increasing the flow of information generally—is rippling through the world economy. For corporations, this will mean less pricing power but also lower overhead, raw material costs, and manufacturing expenses. For consumers, the net effect (pardon the pun) will be not just greater convenience but also cheaper prices— or at least a slowdown in the rate at which prices rise.

Federal Reserve Board Chairman Alan Greenspan is one of many noted economists who have repeatedly cited the advent of the Internet as one of the most significant aspects of the high-technology revolution. That revolution, Mr. Greenspan says, has fundamentally changed the way the global economy operates, improving efficiency, increasing productivity, and helping to hold inflation in check. Mr. Greenspan is willing to take this argument only so far, however. He notes, for example, that other factors have at times acted as inflation stimulants—including the occasionally incredible values of Internet and technology stocks that make investors *feel* richer and thus spend more money. But other economists take the argument much further, suggesting that the Internet and other advances have practically eliminated inflation in the United States by holding down the cost of raw materials, and by making it hard for retailers to raise prices. The Net, after all, is the ultimate tool for comparison shoppers, with whole businesses devoted to helping e-shoppers find the lowest price for any product with just a few keystrokes. "The Internet is more important than the Fed," writes economist Larry Kudlow of ING Barings and CNBC.com. "Easily accessible low-cost information and increased competition, the hallmarks of Internet economics, will contribute substantially more growth with significantly lower prices. Think of it as *deflationary growth*, a classic consequence of long-wave technology cycles. This is the new paradigm of the information economy."

There is, of course, a downside to all these positive developments. For all those new businesses that have sprung up out of nowhere, for all the convenience the Net has meant to consumers, for all the efficiencies it has created for companies and the inflation-fighting effects it has had on the economy—the Net has also endangered countless old-world companies and threatened to displace millions of jobs. In some cases, those businesses that are jeopardized simply have little reason to exist in a Webified world. Once consumers can search for the cheapest, most convenient airline tickets, car rentals, and hotel reservations with just the touch of a

few buttons, for example, why use traditional travel agents? Once
publishers and record labels can distribute books and music on-line,
on demand, why would anybody want to rummage around in traditional bookstores or record shops? Once individuals can put their
basement clutter up for sale before a global audience, fetching un-
thinkable prices for otherwise worthless tchatchkes, why would
they ever want to rely on traditional newspaper classifieds? This, in
a word, is disintermediation: the act of removing the middleman.
The tremendous commercial power of the Net—to heighten convenience, improve efficiency, and keep prices low—derives precisely
from the fact that it is the greatest disintermediator the world has
ever known. It threatens to do to thousands of businesses and their
employees what the electric refrigerator did to the iceman.

As with previous technological revolutions, however—from
the advent of electricity to the invention of the microchip—those
companies that survive will ultimately be strengthened. Thus,
companies from General Motors to General Electric—if their efforts at Webification are successful—could in theory get better
prices on thousands of component parts that go into every product
they make, while improving the efficiency of their just-in-time
manufacturing systems by having computers automatically monitor inventories and reorder supplies as needed. The result should be
fatter profit margins—assuming that GM and GE are able to maintain some degree of pricing power over their customers. But even if
they aren't—because the same Internet that allows them to comparison shop for cheaper widgets allows their customers to comparison shop for cars and dishwashers—these companies will
nonetheless be better off for embracing the Web early and will gain
an advantage over rivals who don't. The Net "is the final nail in the
coffin of bureaucracy," says legendary GE Chairman Jack Welch.
"It's taken the company by storm. It's exciting, it's faster. Business
will never be the same again."

The Internet and You

All this said, the Net is also a barrel of misconceptions. It isn't just
four or five years old, for example. It's been around for nearly

thirty years—though it's only recently become a means of doing business (more on this in a moment). "Internet companies" aren't just newly fledged, profitless enterprises run by technogeeks fresh out of college. There are some of those, to be sure, but there are also plenty of mainstream, very large, and very profitable companies that are central players in the Internet. And the Internet hasn't redefined investing. Despite all the Net lingo about things such as "eyeballs," "stickiness," and "virality," the key "metric"—a term that is itself Net jargon for "measurement"—remains, as it has for centuries, corporate profitability. Rest assured, no company without profits can exist indefinitely. Finally, and most important, the Internet isn't nearly as risky as you and many other investors may think. The Internet is such a mainstream phenomenon that the riskiest investment strategy may be avoiding it rather than embracing it.

Just how the Internet and all the companies associated with it fit into your personal portfolio is something that only you can determine. You can, for example, choose to play with the fast money that tries to determine which sector or subsector of the Net will be the next hot theme. Stocks in whatever sector that is will be extremely volatile; initial public offerings of companies in the category will skyrocket in a matter of minutes. The gains to be made are spectacular. But so are the losses. If you choose to take part in that mad scramble, don't call yourself an investor. You're a speculator, and you are playing a very risky game.

At the other end of the spectrum you can be content to pay little attention to the Internet or Internet stocks. Invest your money for the long haul in index funds, and relax secure in the knowledge that as the Internet grows to encompass virtually every aspect of the domestic and global economy you'll be along for the ride. Already, for example, the Standard & Poor's 500 stock index sports two very prominent Internet companies—AOL Time Warner and Yahoo!—and dozens of other companies in the index, while still classified as "old-economy" firms, are rapidly remaking themselves to take advantage of the efficiencies the Internet offers. Take this approach, and I can guarantee you won't make the kind of fabulous profits that the speculators are after. But you almost certainly won't suffer catastrophic losses either. If the Internet is indeed ushering in a new era of prosperity and productivity, a diversified portfolio of U.S. and foreign stocks will reflect those improving economic circumstances.

Then there's the vast middle ground between those extremes, a rich array of stocks and mutual funds that let anyone tailor a portfolio to suit his or her own needs. Somewhere amid all those offerings is where I figure you'll want to be. I'm assuming that you know the fundamentals of investing: the importance of a diversified portfolio, the costs of commissions and taxes, and the essential metrics (there's that word again) of stock evaluation: revenues, profits, and price-earnings ratios, for example. If you don't feel completely comfortable in that arena of stock evaluation, don't worry. I'll explain a lot of that as we go along. If you're new enough to investing to be uncertain about concepts such as diversification and the impact of costs on returns, you probably should stop here and go find a good explanation of what investing is all about. And if you want to play at either of the extremes I mentioned earlier, you can stop here, too. This isn't a text about gambling, and if you're just buying index funds you certainly don't need the information in the remainder of this book (though, of course, you *may* find it interesting). But if you want to take advantage of the Internet in your own portfolio, read on.

A Little Background

Although what we know as the Internet entered our consciousness in the 1990s, the Net was born nearly three decades earlier as part of a federal cost-cutting program. At the time, computers were massive, room-sized machines costing millions of dollars each and used mostly for government research, although a few universities owned them, too. Many of those universities obtained their computers through government grants. That led a federal bureaucrat at the Advanced Research Projects Agency (ARPA) to the conclusion in the late 1960s that the government could save lots of money by enabling universities to share computer power among themselves. It was a radical notion, given that the technology didn't yet exist for two computers in the same room to talk to each other, much less to share information with other computers hundreds or even thousands of miles away. Solving that problem became a challenge that, by some accounts, rivaled the effort to put a man on the moon. And in fact, at around the same time that Neil Armstrong was stepping onto the lunar surface, the first crude messages began passing back and forth among computers in four locations in California and Utah. By 1970, the first East Coast branch of this new computer network was established in Cambridge, Massachusetts. And gradually, the ARPANET, as it became known, expanded to include dozens, and later hundreds, of locations all across the country. In 1973, computers in England and Norway were connected. And while the system was first used to perform complex research, it very quickly became a means of communication as well, with the first e-mail messages transmitted by the early 1970s.

The immense efficiencies inherent in sharing computer power at long distances touched off the creation of dozens of other computer networks around the country, at universities, government agencies, and even some companies. Each of these networks operated differently from the others, with different computers speaking different languages. The result: a cacophony of small networks that couldn't share information with one another. And that problem touched off yet another quest for a solution, one that was solved by the mid-1980s, when technology was created that allowed the different networks to communicate with one another. The product of this "inter-networking of networks": the Internet.

During this entire time, the Net remained a text-based medium, with nothing in the way of graphics and few practical applications beyond communications and computer and mathematical research. It was extremely user-unfriendly, with only the most computer-savvy of individuals able to figure out how to use it. But those advances, too, came quickly. In 1990, a computer scientist in Switzerland created the World Wide Web—a system of addresses and common standards that simplified the way users of the Net could find one another. The Web also allowed computers on the Net to pass information back and forth using an agreed-upon set of rules, so that the information looks the same no matter what type of computer is accessing it. From that point on, developments piled one on top of the other. In 1992, led by then-Senator Albert Gore,

Jr., Congress passed a law that opened the so-called Information Superhighway for uses beyond research and education, helping to foster the growth of commerce on this exploding medium. In 1993, several graduate students at the University of Illinois invented the first "browser," a piece of software that makes it little more than child's play to navigate the Web and view information graphically.

Within a year, the browser software created in Illinois—initially called Mosaic but later renamed Netscape Navigator—was the basis of a company, Netscape Communications, and the trigger that led to the Internet's spectacular growth. Netscape went public a year after that in a hugely successful initial public stock offering that ushered in the age of Internet stock euphoria. In 1994, a Wall Street denizen named Jeff Bezos became one of the first to realize the commercial applications of this fast-growing new medium and set out to capitalize on them. His on-line bookstore, Amazon.com, was launched in 1995. It went public in its own hot IPO just two years after that and within a few years became a place to buy virtually anything on-line—not just books, compact discs, and videos, but also toys, toasters, and even chain saws. Hard on its heels followed the creation of hundreds of other Internet businesses: book stores, toy stores, drug stores, wine shops, sporting goods stores, pet supplies stores, and on and on. Thus the Internet was transformed from a communications medium into a medium for commerce, and Internet stocks became—overnight, it seemed—the hottest form of investment in anyone's recent memory.

Is It My Eyes, or Are These Distinctions Blurring?

In the earliest days of the Internet as we know it today—that is, about seven years ago—there were Internet companies that either did business on the Net or helped make it possible for others, and there was everybody else. But that distinction has faded considerably since and will be essentially meaningless in a few years. The borders between what is and what isn't an Internet business are rapidly blurring as more and more companies, both old and new, do business on the Net. Some use the Net mostly to simplify and streamline their back-office processes, such as purchasing. Others use it as an additional channel for communicating and doing business with customers, just as they would the telephone or a physical store. A few do business mostly or exclusively on-line, but they are, and will remain, a minority. Many of the dot coms that began life as Web sites have started to open physical locations, to team with bricks-and-mortar counterparts, or in some other way to develop tangible, physical embodiments of their virtual selves.

Examples abound of how the world of Internet companies and the old economy are blending. Take, for example, Amazon.com. There isn't any question that it's an Internet company. It sells products exclusively on-line and operates no "real-world" bricks-and-mortar stores. But it also owns millions of dollars worth of physical inventory, stockpiled in cavernous distribution centers around the world—complete with conveyer belts, forklifts, and thousands of employees. And it has a joint venture with Toys "R" Us, under which Amazon sells and distributes an inventory of children's products selected, and owned, by Toys "R" Us.

Then there's eBay. It, too, is unquestionably an Internet company. It does business mostly on-line, owns no inventory, and its person-to-person auction business couldn't have existed before the Internet. But eBay also owns a real-world auction house, Butterfields, that has been around for more than a century.

Now consider AT&T. It is the country's largest long-distance phone company, as well as its largest cable television provider, with tens of thousands of employees and a massive physical infrastructure that stretches from coast to coast. But its network is also one of the largest carriers of Internet data traffic (the Web's circulatory system), and it controls the nation's largest high-speed Internet access service. It may not be a pure Internet play, but the Internet is a huge and growing part of its business. Indeed, the decline of Ma Bell's core long-distance business and the rise of the Net are key reasons behind the company's dramatic restructuring and breakup, announced in late 2000 and expected to occur over several years.

Finally, look at General Motors, which builds and sells cars and trucks, one of the most inventory-intensive and labor-intensive industries around. But GM is also a part owner of what is expected to become one of the world's largest on-line purchasing exchanges, and it will soon buy most of its billions of dollars worth of supplies over the Net. It's far from a pure Internet play, but there isn't any question that the Internet will play a critical role in the company's future.

All this probably sounds a little confusing, and the last thing I want to do is confuse you. So if you're willing to accept that the distinctions between what is and what isn't an Internet company are a bit arbitrary, I will, for the purposes of this book, define an "Internet company" as one that derives most of its revenue from transactions completed over the Net or whose business is predominantly and inextricably related to the Net. But I'm not going to ignore the many companies that, while not deriving the bulk of their revenues on-line, nevertheless stand to benefit in some notable or significant way from doing *more* of their business on the Net or, more indirectly, from the explosion in *other* companies doing business on-line.

The aim of creating these distinctions—and there are more detailed distinctions yet to come—is to give you the tools you need not only to analyze various companies as potential investments, but also to allow you to analyze your own investment portfolio. Only by understanding the broad categories, such as Internet companies and non-Internet companies, and more detailed categories among the Internet companies, will you be able to control and achieve the proper exposure to this new investment opportunity. Believe me, too much exposure to the Internet can be just as dangerous as too little.

Categories and Subcategories

Wall Street tends to group Internet stocks into three broad categories:

- Business-to-consumer (known as "B2C") companies aim their products or services at individual customers such as you and me.

- Business-to-business ("B2B") companies sell their products and services to other companies.
- Infrastructure companies (sorry, no catchy nickname) focus on building the physical components of the Net.

We'll use that basic system in this book, although you should understand that, like the differences between Internet and non-Internet companies, the distinctions between these subcategories can become blurry, too. Most infrastructure companies are, in some sense, B2B companies as well, since their customers are other companies, not retail consumers. Some companies cross several boundaries. AOL Time Warner, for example, is partly an infrastructure company, since as an Internet service provider it operates a large telecommunications infrastructure that is part of the Net's physical backbone. But AOL is also a B2C company, since it aims most of its products and services at consumers and operates a consumer-oriented "portal" that serves as the virtual gateway to the Web for tens of millions of people. Yahoo!, meanwhile, is predominantly a B2C company, since the vast majority of its services are consumer-oriented. But it is increasingly targeting the business of helping other companies build and operate Web sites in exchange for a fee or a percentage of sales.

Despite the increasing blurriness of all the categories, you can tell a lot about the challenges and opportunities facing an Internet company by determining which category it falls under. An infrastructure company such as Cisco Systems, for example, has a smaller number of potential customers than a B2C powerhouse such as Amazon.com. As a result, Cisco has a lot less reason to invest in a massive, coast-to-coast advertising campaign to build its brand name than does Amazon. On the other hand, Amazon isn't actually building machines, nor does it have too much to fear from new technological innovations that could put it out of business; but this is a very real threat to Cisco. As a result, Cisco has more reason to invest in research and development than does Amazon. On the revenue side, Cisco's customers are buying a relatively small number of big-ticket items from the company, and those items can't be found in too many other places; Amazon's customers, on the other hand, are buying a relatively large number of small-ticket items from the company, and those are things they could probably find at many other stores. Thus the competitive situation of the two companies' respective markets and the resulting profit margins on the items they sell look different and must be analyzed differently. Those differences will become much more apparent in subsequent chapters.

CHAPTER TWO

You've Got Scale!

AOL Time Warner:
A Paradigm of the New Economy

THE YEAR 2000 was little more than a week old when Americans awoke to the news of a stunning corporate marriage: America Online, a company dreamed up less than two decades earlier, was buying Time Warner, the world's largest media conglomerate, in the largest takeover in American history—a deal worth more than $140 billion at the time it was announced. Barely eight years after going public—barely three years after it was derided as "America On Hold" by observers who ridiculed its technology as unsophisticated and unreliable—AOL had pulled off a remarkable corporate coup. Using as currency a high-flying stock skeptics regarded as overvalued and headed for collapse, it had acquired one of the most respected and enduring icons of the media world—a company that traced its origins to the early part of the twentieth century and that counted among its assets some of the most prestigious media brands in existence. AOL had delivered a kick in the pants to the legions of cynics and naysayers who belittled the Internet's significance and groused about the valuations Wall Street was placing on dot-com companies. And it had become the ultimate symbol of the new economy's triumph over the old, a symbolism made all the more powerful by the fact that it coincided precisely with the dawning of a new millennium.

On its surface, the deal seemed as unlikely a pairing of corporate cultures and assets as was possible. Operating out of a sprawling campus in suburban Virginia, AOL was, like its Silicon Valley peers on the opposite coast, a laid-back place where suits and ties were rare but multimillion-dollar brokerage accounts weren't, where an entrepreneurial passion for creating something from nothing seemed to permeate the atmosphere, from the lowliest new hire to the most senior executive. Yet for all the enormous value Wall Street had placed on the company—and for all the enormous wealth that had been created among its ranks—AOL had few real-world assets to speak of. It didn't "make" anything. It didn't "own" much more than its name and the server computers required to operate its service. Most of its customers had been with the company for little more than a year or two. And its financial position—while the envy of the Internet world—was insignificant by big-company standards: profits of just $681 million on revenues of $5.8 billion in calendar year 1999.

Time Warner, by contrast—headquartered in a high-rise building in the heart of New York City—was a buttoned-down place where bureaucrats were many and innovators few, where most employees worked nine-to-five jobs for decent paychecks but true wealth was, as at most Fortune 500 companies, confined to the uppermost ranks of the executive suite. Its assets were considerable: brands ranging from Time and Warner Brothers to CNN and HBO, among others; leading positions in the worlds of magazine publishing, film production, television production, and music distribution; and the second largest cable television system in the country, with lines passing through more than 20 million homes. And its income statement made AOL look positively anemic: profits of $7.3 billion in 1999 on revenues of more than $27 billion.

Announcing the merger in the Grand Ballroom of New York's Waldorf-Astoria Hotel that January morning, executives of the two companies went to almost comical lengths to downplay these differences. Time Warner's graying chairman, Gerald Levin—the

CEO of the combined company—looked out of place wearing the open-necked blue shirt that is the unofficial uniform of Silicon Valley. Meanwhile, AOL's boyish-looking chairman, Steve Case—the chairman of the new firm—had made sure to dress up in a conservative dark suit and tie.

The executives didn't need to try so hard. On closer examination, the combination of this old-world behemoth with this new-economy titan makes so much sense in so many ways that it almost seems predestined. And by some accounts, it was. Years before most people had heard of his company, Mr. Case was telling associates that AOL would one day rank among the world's largest and most powerful media companies. That remark—brazen and wildly optimistic at the time it was made—was temporarily forgotten amid the stock market's love affair with "pure-play" dot coms, when old-economy companies such as Time Warner saw their stocks punished for not "getting it" about the Net and real-world assets seemed almost a ball and chain that weighed companies down unnecessarily. But it was nonetheless prescient. Arrogant as his statement was, Mr. Case was not as arrogant as the dot-com disciples who believed the Internet would rewrite, from scratch, the rules of business success. And he wasn't as arrogant as the old-economy veterans who refused to understand the ways in which the Net was changing their world. Rather, Mr. Case recognized that the old and new economies had much to gain from each other—a lesson for which his company, AOL Time Warner, stands as a prime example.

Chinks in the Armor

Why did AOL and Time Warner need each other? After all, at the time of the merger, both companies seemed at the top of their game. AOL held a dominating position in the Internet service provider business, with well over 20 million customers and a hammerlock on 50 percent of the market. It was one of the few profitable Internet companies, and its revenues were growing at nearly 30 percent a year. Time Warner, meanwhile, was a commanding presence in film, music, television, and magazine publishing. Its cable television operation, second only in size to the amalgam of cable assets cobbled together by AT&T, was of increasing value as investors recognized that those cables held the promise of carrying not just one-way TV signals but also two-way telephone and Internet traffic.

But that rosy picture masked mounting weaknesses at both firms. AOL, for one, faced growing competition on one side from rivals that were giving away Internet service for free, and on the other side from premium Internet access providers that were offering a high-speed, always-on (also known as "broadband") connection to the Web that was far superior to AOL's slower dial-up, or "narrowband," service. Though AOL had formed alliances with Hughes DirecTV satellite service, as well as with various regional Bell operating companies, to access their high-speed connections into millions of American homes, it still lacked a comprehensive broadband strategy or even the ability to deliver high-speed access to most of its *existing* customers. In short, AOL risked being squeezed out—its subscription fees eroded by the low-cost providers on one side, its most active customers poached by the premium-priced broadband services on the other.

AOL also lacked content. Much of the company's success until the merger is explained by the fact that, within its own proprietary network, AOL offers much of the information people go on-line to obtain. AOL customers can—without ever leaving the AOL network—use either standard e-mail or "instant" messaging to communicate with other AOL members, buy movie tickets, manage their daily calendar and their personal finances, shop at a variety of on-line stores, and, of course, access all sorts of news and information. While AOL also allows customers to access the World Wide Web, many do so only infrequently, spending the bulk of their hour-plus a day on-line within AOL's "walled garden"—some without even realizing that they aren't on the Web.

That ability to keep users within the confines of its proprietary service gives AOL a huge advantage in selling advertising. Quite simply, the more time AOL customers spend within the service, the more time they're likely to spend looking at ads or buying goods from AOL's partners; conversely, once they leave the network, AOL has no way of making money off them. But keeping users within its own service requires providing them with content—ideally, the type of content they can't get anywhere else. The more of that content AOL can provide, the less users will look for it elsewhere. Since the premerger AOL didn't actually produce any of its own content, it was paying third parties to provide such content for it, to the tune of about $150 million a year.

For its part, Time Warner lacked any meaningful presence on the Internet—though not for want of trying. The company had invested—and planned to continue investing—hundreds of millions of dollars in building a series of on-line outlets for its off-line content, centered around a single Web site, Pathfinder, that would act as a "portal," or gateway, to all the others. But Pathfinder had failed to catch on with consumers, suffering from a clunky design and the lack of an identifiable brand. And even within the company, for all the money that was being thrown at it, Time Warner's on-line efforts were embraced only halfheartedly and weren't part of a larger vision of how to utilize the Web.

In this regard, Time Warner pre-AOL wasn't all that different from a host of other media giants—from Disney to NBC to CBS—that felt they needed some sort of Internet presence but weren't sure what to do about that. Most of these companies came late to the Web and were thus doomed to play catch-up from the very beginning. Several went out and bought existing Web sites—Disney acquired Infoseek and NBC bought Xoom.com, among others—but they tried to do so on the cheap, and the sites they bought weren't leaders in their respective categories and weren't particularly well integrated with the on-line and off-line content the acquirers already had.

In part, though, the problems confronted by Time Warner, Disney, and their peers weren't really their fault. For one thing, as investors swarmed over Internet stocks and drove their valuations to unprecedented levels, they left old-line media companies by the wayside. That had a double-whammy effect, making potential acquisition targets hugely expensive, even as it made any would-be big media acquirer's currency relatively less valuable. At the same time, the lack of a dot-com currency made it difficult to attract the best talent to grow any Web presence from within. Why, after all, work hard to build a Web site for Time Warner when you could build the same kind of Web site for some Silicon Valley start-up—perhaps your own start-up—and become rich beyond your wildest dreams in the process? For those who did decide to stay with a giant such as Time Warner, the entrepreneurial spirit and get-rich-quick incentive simply weren't there in the same way. Finally, there was the matter of how much red ink a big company could stomach. For start-ups, red ink wasn't a problem during most of the Internet stock frenzy, as investors were willing to look the other way in anticipation of huge profits years down the road. (This atmosphere ultimately changed, in early 2000, but it did so only *after* Time Warner agreed to be bought by AOL, not before.) For existing non-dot-com companies, on the other hand—backed as they were by a whole different class of investors—red ink was taboo. Ironically, then, their deep pockets were of little help. The companies were thus doubly cursed: not only weren't they awarded Internet-type valuations, but they were also discouraged from making the types of investments necessary to build an Internet presence by investors who frowned on anything that dampened the bottom line.

What's more, these three issues—the lack of a dot-com currency, the lack of ability to recruit the best dot-com talent, and the inability to make the types of massive investments required to build a dot-com presence—dogged not just media companies such as Time Warner, Disney, Viacom, and NBC but essentially every giant of the old economy. Wal-Mart, Kmart, and Toys "R" Us all encountered similar troubles on their road to the Net. Of these, only Time Warner went so far as to merge with a dot-com company—a move that only barely predated the tech-stock sell-off of 2000. That sell-off—which narrowed the gap between dot-com and traditional company valuations—helped reduce the relative disadvantage faced by old-economy giants to some extent, though the troubles these companies encountered early in their on-line efforts continue to dog them to varying degrees.

A Match Made in Heaven?

If they seemed, in their heritage and culture, utterly mismatched, AOL and Time Warner did, in coming together, offset each other's weaknesses and enhance each other's strengths in important ways —at least in theory. (Their marriage is young enough that it's still far from clear whether they'll be able to avoid the huge execution pitfalls inherent in megamergers.) At the simplest level, the deal provides AOL an enormous revenue base and multiple revenue streams—both of which it previously lacked—giving the company the scale and strength to withstand a downturn in any one line of business. For example, the erosion in dial-up Internet access rates caused by the rise of free Internet access—once a very real threat to AOL's business model and its business—is now a considerably smaller threat, since Internet subscription revenues have become a vastly smaller portion of the combined company's business. Overall, subscription revenues will contribute about 40 percent of the company's total revenues in the first few years of the union, compared with about 80 percent for the premerger AOL. What's more, those subscription revenues aren't just Internet-related; they also include Time Warner's publications and cable assets.

Perhaps more important strategically, the missing link in AOL's broadband strategy—its lack of a high-speed link into millions of homes—was immediately filled by Time Warner's cable assets. The combined AOL Time Warner is now the nation's second largest cable operator, and thus the second largest owner of that critical broadband link. Between its joint ventures with DirecTV and various Baby Bells, and its own cable systems, AOL Time Warner can now try to convert many of its existing dial-up Internet access customers to a more expensive high-speed service, even as it can sell new Internet access services to millions of Time Warner customers with whom it now has cable TV relationships. Of course, the combined company won't be allowed to keep rivals off of its cable lines, so it won't have exclusive access to those customers. But its ownership of the distribution infrastructure puts it in an enviable position nonetheless; it will make money either from the rival ISPs, which must pay to use its cable lines to provide their services, or by using those lines itself. In addition, it will be in a stronger position to negotiate distribution deals with other infrastructure owners for access to their pipes.

For its part, Time Warner's missing, or at least underdeveloped, Internet strategy was immediately strengthened by the deal in ways that would have taken the company many years and many hundreds of millions of dollars to accomplish on its own—assuming that would even have been possible. Not only has Time Warner gained access to some of the best on-line assets in the Internet world, but it has gained the management talent that built those assets—a talent it sorely lacked. Before the merger, Time Warner risked falling further and further behind in the race to develop an Internet presence and an on-line distribution outlet for its content. With the merger, it was instantly catapulted into the media industry's on-line pole position.

Beyond standard Internet access, AOL's merger with Time Warner should speed the development and rollout of interactive television. This union of TV and the Internet was a goal of the pre-merger AOL. While it's true that there has been a dramatic increase in the time Americans spend in front of their computers, they still spend six or seven times as many hours in front of their TV sets. The notion of turning the TV into an Internet appliance is a logical one—allowing users to chat on-line with one another while watching a show, for example, to find out more information about a program they're watching, or even to order products right off the TV screen, thus enhancing TV's potential application as a retail outlet. Imagine watching the latest installment of *Who Wants to Be a Millionaire?* and being able to play along with your friends as they watch in their own homes—or with millions of other people watching across the country. Imagine further being able to click on Regis Philbin's necktie with your mouse and instantly call up its designer and price—and then, with another couple of clicks, order it! The combination of AOL with Time Warner has made this type of interactivity a much more likely near-term phenomenon.

The merger also gives AOL access to Time Warner's vast trove of proprietary content—from articles in *Time* magazine to original movies created for HBO to music distributed by Warner Records—and its repertoire of recognized brand names. Recall that proprietary content was one of the features that gave rise to AOL's success as an ISP. It stands to reason, then, that having more of it should enhance that success. At the very least, AOL will now have to pay less for its content, since any Time Warner content it was paying for is now free, and content from many other providers can probably be replaced by Time Warner content.

What's more, beyond ordinary text-based content, AOL now

has access to Time Warner's film and music output. Listening to and downloading music has become popular on the Web only recently, and the streaming or downloading of films is still in its infancy. But as faster, higher-quality broadband service becomes the norm—and as television and the Internet converge—the ability to access music and films should become an ever more important reason for going on-line. The combined AOL Time Warner is perfectly positioned to take advantage of this situation, with the company owning not just one of the world's largest libraries of such content but also the infrastructure to deliver it to the end user. Bob Pittman, the former president of AOL and now the co–chief operating officer of the combined AOL Time Warner, compares the combined company's potential impact on the music industry to the impact of the compact disc in the 1980s. That development, which made recorded music easier and better to listen to, helped expand the music market and drive sales higher. Distributing music on-line could have a similar effect by broadening the audience of potential customers and making it easier to find and buy the music those customers are interested in, easier to access it from multiple locations, and cheaper and easier for a company such as AOL Time Warner to market it to potential customers. Mr. Pittman should know. At the time the CD was revolutionizing the music industry, he was at the heart of the revolution as one of the creators of MTV. But the same logic goes for movies, particularly with the advent of AOL TV. Imagine being able to type into your television set the name of any movie you wish to watch, at any time, and download it to your TV for a small fee. Not only does that possibility threaten to wipe out the video store, chances are it would also encourage you to watch movies more frequently (no longer would you need to drag yourself out to the store to see if the movie you want is available—only to find that it isn't!). As a result, the combination of AOL and Time Warner portends the possibility of a faster-growing market for Time Warner's music and film assets. At the same time, customers will have more reason to access the AOL service and less reason to wander beyond it, making AOL that much more of an attractive outlet for advertisers.

Indeed, advertising is yet another way in which the merger stands to benefit both companies, giving both sides new opportunities to cross-sell advertisers on different platforms and to package advertising in ways that weren't previously possible. AOL, for example, can now offer its advertisers deals on TV and magazine advertising, while Time Warner can offer its clients deals on on-line advertising and open the doors for AOL to a whole set of clients that may never previously have considered the Internet as an advertising outlet. If each company separately was a "must-have" advertising destination in the various media they dominated, the combined company is an even more important advertising destination across many media—and its negotiating position has been strengthened as a result. Time Warner's on-line properties, for example—which before the merger were an unremarkable destination for advertisers and an insignificant source of advertising revenue—became instantly more appealing as a part of AOL's dominant on-line network.

Potentially even more compelling to advertisers is the ability for a combined AOL Time Warner to know more about its customers than either company knew individually. For example, while AOL might previously have known a great deal about its members' on-line habits and interests, it knew nothing about their off-line habits. Now that AOL and Time Warner are part of the same family, an AOL advertiser may be able to target, quite specifically, an AOL member who also subscribes to a Time Warner magazine— say, *Sports Illustrated*—while a *Sports Illustrated* advertiser may be able to target an AOL customer who is interested in sports but isn't a *Sports Illustrated* subscriber.

Similar cross-selling opportunities are available on the consumer side of the new company's various businesses. When AOL customers go on-line, for example, they can now be peppered with offers for Time Warner's various magazines or promotions for its movies. Time Warner customers can, in similar fashion, be encouraged to use AOL's Internet service. And various services can be bundled together in appealing packages that weren't previously possible.

Finally, the merger offers a host of cost-saving opportunities, though these pale in importance compared with its potential to generate new revenues. Besides the obvious synergies in areas such as corporate overhead—public relations, human resources, accounting, and so forth—there are more subtle ways a combined AOL Time Warner can save money. Would-be subscribers to Time Warner's cable service or its various magazines, for example, can now be asked to sign up on-line, allowing the company to scale back its more expensive human-run customer service operations. Even more significant over the short term, Time Warner, which had planned to spend several hundred million dollars on developing and promoting its Internet assets, can now pare that spending back considerably. And one of AOL's biggest expenses—the cost of providing its service over other companies' telecommunications infrastructure—can gradually be reduced as its services migrate to the Time Warner cable network.

It's Not All Wine and Roses

As with any giant merger, there are serious potential downsides to the deal that could undermine all its potential strengths. Some of these drawbacks are obvious, others might emerge quite quickly in the months after the merger, while still others could take years to become apparent. For example, after the merger of Time and Warner in 1989, the combined company's stock stayed in a funk for close to eight years as the two firms struggled mightily to make the combination successful.

The most immediate threat is of clashes at the executive level, with executives from both sides vying for control of the combined entity. Though it was financially structured as a takeover of Time Warner by AOL, AOL Time Warner officials have stressed that the combination is actually a "merger of equals," with managers picked from both sides based purely on merit. In point of fact, however, mergers of equals almost never work out that way. In AOL Time Warner's case, it seems unlikely that the company's initial structure—with a chairman from the AOL side and a chief executive officer from the Time Warner side both reporting independently to an equally divided board of directors, along with two coequal chief operating officers, one from each side—will last very long. In the short term, the threat is of stalemate, with the decision-making pace slowed by the unwieldy structure at the top. Over the longer term, it's likely that one side—chances are, AOL—will emerge as the dominant force in the relationship, with its managers assuming control over key areas. That in turn is likely to lead to an exodus of senior executives from the other side. And in fact, a notable feature of the financial structure of this particular merger is that the stock options of Time Warner employees vested—or became immediately exercisable—upon the signing of the deal, while the options for AOL employees won't vest until January 2002. As the merger led to considerable wealth creation for Time Warner shareholders, since that company was bought out at a premium, this vesting structure leads to an even greater likelihood of an exodus from the Time Warner side of the operation.

Beyond the risk of disagreements in the executive suite, there is the threat of a broader cultural clash throughout the organization. That's particularly true in a combination such as this one, which brings together not just two companies of different sizes and different histories but also two entirely different industries. It's probably safe to say that, by and large, AOL employees are younger, wealthier (thanks to stock options), and more entrepreneurial than their Time Warner counterparts. Thus it isn't hard to imagine that the Time Warner side could bridle at the notion of taking direction from young upstarts in Virginia or that the AOL side could find itself stymied by the bureaucracy in New York.

Even assuming that culture clash is not a big problem, there is the risk that AOL Time Warner will find itself unable to execute on the vision or potential of the combined company. At the most basic level, that company is now far bigger and more complex than either firm was before. Beyond that, though, this deal, as it was described by executives from both sides, was not predominantly about wringing cost savings or efficiencies out of bringing the two organizations together. Rather, it was about adding one and one together and creating three, by taking the strengths and expertise of either side and then growing the combined business faster than either individual company could grow its own business. But it's a long way from such a vision to its realization. What if AOL is unable to make as much out of Time Warner's Internet operations as it hopes to? What if advertising or subscription cross-selling efforts don't work out as well as planned? Or what if market conditions change in such a way that AOL's subscription revenues dry up more quickly than expected, or the advertising market slows down faster than anticipated (as it did in late 2000 and early 2001), or another competitor (a combined Yahoo!-Disney, for example) emerges to compete with the combined entity more intensely than any rival does now? While the executives from both sides have experience integrating mergers, they don't have experience with a merger of this scale, and execution is a paramount factor in any business combination.

Finally, from a strictly financial perspective, there's no question that AOL's revenue and profit growth rates will slow considerably from what they were, though both numbers will be growing off of a much bigger base. Before the merger, for example, AOL's revenues were growing at an estimated annual rate of nearly 30 percent, while its cash earnings (before deductions for interest, taxes, depreciation, and amortization—an accounting measure referred to as EBITDA, or cash flow, and commonly used for Internet and media companies) were growing at an annual rate of 50 percent. Time Warner's revenues, by contrast, were projected to grow by just 6 percent per year over the long term, while its cash earnings were projected to grow by 12 percent. With the bulk of its revenues and earnings coming from the slower-growing Time Warner side, AOL Time Warner is likely to see its revenues grow at an annual rate in the midteens (in percentage terms), while its cash earnings will grow in the mid–20 to 30 percent range for some time. While executives stress that the combination should lead to faster growth in every area of the business than was the case before the merger, simple math dictates that the *rate* of growth will be slower for the much bigger AOL Time Warner than it was for the much smaller AOL.

This slower growth rate isn't necessarily a problem. What it does mean is that investors who bought AOL's stock because it was such a rapidly growing company are now likely to be less interested in AOL Time Warner, since its growth rate will be about half that of AOL alone. Taken together with the fact that it is now a much bigger company, with a bigger market value and many more shares of stock outstanding, shares of the combined AOL Time Warner are likely to appreciate at a slower rate than shares of AOL alone. Consider the simple fact that before the merger, AOL had about 2.3 billion shares of stock outstanding and that, after the merger, the combined company has about 4.5 billion shares outstanding. Simple math tells you it'll take a lot more trading action to move the stock. That's not to say, by any means, that the company is a bad investment. It simply means that the days of hypergrowth—as well as hypervolatility—are likely behind it and that future investors aren't likely to "get rich quick" on AOL's stock the way investors might have in the company's earlier days.

What Does It All Add Up To?

Assuming that the combined company's management *is* able to execute on the deal's potential and make AOL Time Warner one of the most important companies in the on-line *or* off-line worlds, there is still the very thorny question of how much the company is worth. Rule number one of investing—a rule we'll revisit later in this book—is that every company is worth different things to different people. For some investors it might make sense to pay a great deal for a particular stock, while others can't justify taking the risk. That said, however, the combined AOL Time Warner is particularly difficult to value against any objective standard because there is no objective standard to compare it to. There simply never has been a company with the same collection of assets, so it's tough to figure out what that collection of assets is worth.

While I'll explore the subject of valuation at much greater length in Chapter Seven, I can establish a few basic points about it right here. First, the value of a company is, and always has been, what investors are willing to pay today for the profits they expect that company to deliver in the future. In recent years, there's been a lot of talk about new valuation measures in the Internet sector, including all sorts of measures of a Web site's popularity or its revenue growth, with lots of fancy names attached to them. These measures aren't meaningless, and I'll explore some of them at more length later. But one thing that should be absolutely clear is this: they are not replacements for the basic principle of profitability. For unprofitable companies, measures of popularity or revenue growth can serve as guideposts to help us figure out how much money a company is likely to earn in future years (a popular Web site, with many users who spend a great deal of time on the site, for example, is likely to make more money in future years than an unpopular Web site). But let's not kid ourselves: over the long run, a company is worth nothing unless it makes money.

In AOL Time Warner's case, the company's cash earnings are generally expected to grow from about $4.3 billion in 2000 to about $18 billion in the year 2006. This estimate—provided by Wall Street analysts who follow the company—is rough and subject to change. It's also, of course, subject to some unpredictable disaster that could spoil the company's profit picture. But at the very least, it gives you some sense of how much money this firm is currently making and is expected to make down the line.

Now comes the all-important question of how much those expected future profits are worth today. Again, we'll delve deeper into this issue in Chapter Seven, but for now two points are critical: what kind of return *you* require over the time you hold the stock and how much of a premium *the rest of the market* is willing to pay for that stock. The first point simply involves determining the return you need to offset the risk you're taking by putting your money to work in the stock. The second requires analyzing the market's psychology, including its willingness to pay much more for faster-growing companies than for slower-growing companies.

For example, *you* might say that to hold AOL Time Warner for the next five years, you will require a steep 22 percent average annual return to offset the risk of holding this particular company over that time and to make up for what else your money could be doing over the same period. Alternatively, you might decide you require a somewhat lower return of, say, 18 percent per year, meaning that you're willing to pay more for the stock. Once you've decided on a number, you can fairly easily determine where the stock would need to be in, say, five years to deliver the kind of return you require—and then it's just a question of whether you think the stock is likely to get there from here. (Alternatively, you can figure out what a company delivering an expected $18 billion in earnings is likely to be worth in 2006 and do the reverse math, discounting that stock price back at your required rate of return until the present. If the stock is trading at or below that level, it meets your price criteria; if it's higher than that level, it's too expensive.)

Figuring out what the *market* is going to be willing to pay for a company delivering $18 billion in earnings several years down the line requires guessing at the *multiple* the market will put on those earnings. For example, for a fast-growing company with a reliable earnings stream, the market might be willing to pay as much as 100 times the following year's expected earnings. But for a slower-growing company, the market may be willing to pay only 30 times the following year's earnings. Another way of thinking about market multiples is in terms of earnings growth rates. For the fastest-growing companies, growth-oriented investors might be willing to apply a premium multiple of as much as twice the companies' annual earnings growth rate, compared with as little as one time that growth rate for slower-growing companies. Thus a company growing its earnings at 50 percent a year might fetch a multiple of 100 times its expected future earnings, while a company growing earnings at 20 percent a year might fetch just 20 or 30 times those expected earnings.

Generally speaking, multiples vary widely across industries and less within a particular industry. For technology-oriented companies, for example, multiples tend to be quite high, because those companies are generally fast-growing and are expected to see continued fast growth for years to come. By the same token, multiples for commercial banks tend to be a lot lower because commercial banking is generally perceived to be a more mature, slower-growing industry.

What makes the case of AOL Time Warner so complicated is that it is partly a fast-growing technology company and partly a slower-growing media company. That makes figuring out a multiple for the stock a bit tricky. Will the market end up valuing the company at the higher end of the range, as more of a tech company, or will it end up valuing it at the lower end of the range, as more of a media company? The difference can be significant. If it values the company as a tech company, and if the company's earnings are really growing in the mid–20 percent range, AOL might rate a multiple in the neighborhood of 50 times its expected future earnings. With $18 billion in expected earnings in the year 2006 and 4.5 billion shares outstanding, simple arithmetic tells you the stock could, under those parameters, fetch as much as $200 in 2005. At a discount rate of 18 percent, that's equal to $103 in 2001. At a discount rate of 22 percent, it's $90. (If you don't understand this math, don't worry —we'll go over another example in greater detail in Chapter Seven.) But if the company is valued as a slower-growing media company— at a multiple of just one time its future growth rate—those numbers look quite different: just $100 a share in 2005 or $52 in 2001 at an 18 percent discount rate, and $48 at a 20 percent discount rate.

So which is the *correct* way of valuing the company? The sad truth is that until things play out in the market, nobody can really know. Perhaps those who value the company as a media company, and thus keep away from it at higher prices, will be proven correct. Perhaps those who are willing to pay more, confident that the market will value it as a leading technology company, will be rewarded for investing now. Some investors who aren't sure suggest splitting the difference, guessing that for several years, the company's value will fall somewhere in between.

If all this confuses you, just leave the math aside for the moment (we'll return to it later) and remember three basic points:

- The value of any company is a function of that company's expected future earnings.
- The market as a whole is willing to pay different types of premiums to own a piece of the earnings of different types of companies—more for faster-growing companies, less for slower-growing companies. (That's why tech stocks are generally more expensive than many other types of stocks.)
- The value of a particular stock to *you* is a function of that company's future earnings, combined with how the market is likely to value those earnings, combined with your own required rate of return. That required rate of return should take into account the risk involved in making the investment and what else your money could be doing in the meantime.

Paradigm of the New Economy?

The good news is that AOL Time Warner isn't likely to be alone for long. If there aren't yet any other companies quite like it, there are likely to be a lot more such companies in the future—not just in the media industry, but across many different industries. That is likely to leave investors somewhat confused for some time, as these companies assume some attributes of fast-growing technology firms while retaining some attributes of their former selves. But however confusing and difficult it may be to ascribe values to them during this period of change, many of these companies, in whatever their industries, are likely to have a few attributes in common with the new AOL Time Warner.

First, the Internet is likely to result in companies that are more vertically integrated than they are today. In the case of AOL Time Warner, for example, not only does the company manufacture content, it also owns the means for that content to be distributed. Soon, instead of buying compact discs manufactured by Warner Music through third-party vendors, you may be able to buy that music directly from AOL Time Warner and have it electronically streamed to you—over cables owned by AOL Time Warner, through a Web site operated by AOL Time Warner—with no middleman in between. Imagine that same situation with books. Instead of buying them from a bookstore, which in turn buys them from a publisher, the publisher might sell them to you directly from its Web site. Or, as mystery maven Stephen King recently attempted in a rather unsuccessful early experiment, the author might eliminate the publisher altogether and sell you the book directly from his own Web site. The same thing could happen to cars. Instead of being forced to trek from dealership to dealership, shopping for the model and price you want, you may be able to negotiate directly with a manufacturer over the Internet, telling General Motors, for example, exactly what you're looking for and finding out, before you ever leave your house, what it'll cost and where you can pick it up. If the middleman isn't totally or immediately eliminated, his role will be gradually and steadily diminished.

Second, the Internet will weave its way through just about every part of most companies' businesses, just as it is weaving its way through every part of the combined AOL Time Warner. The Internet will be a way for companies to sell their product to consumers or to other companies. But it will also be a way for them to communicate internally, to order their own products, and to manage their own supply chains. In other words, both at the front end and at the back end, the Internet will become an integral feature of the way companies across industries do business, and it will make them more efficient.

Finally, the Internet will not just streamline the flow of information, it will also increase the amount and importance of that information. Just as AOL can keep close track of its consumers' on-line habits and match them with their off-line habits as Time Warner customers, targeting them with more appropriate advertising as a result, so too will other companies be able to learn more about their customers' tastes and preferences. When cars are Internet-ready, GM will be able to keep tabs on its customers' driving habits; when books are purchased on-line directly from authors, those authors will be able to contact their readers directly to announce subsequent publications. All this raises concerns about privacy—or the lack thereof—that no doubt will have to be dealt with. But the Internet economy is often called the information economy in part because the Internet has made more information more widely available than ever before. Whatever parameters or restrictions are ultimately placed on the use of that information, there is little doubt that the Net is helping companies and consumers alike become better informed about one another.

Today, these three attributes are unique to a handful of hybrid companies, such as AOL Time Warner, that straddle the old and new economies. For now, though more and more businesses are becoming Internet-savvy—and integrating the Net into their daily practices—the economy remains relatively divided between Internet and non-Internet companies. That, I hope, makes a book like this, which aims to explain the way the Internet economy and the businesses within it work, of some value. But while it's important to understand how these new Internet companies function, it's equally important to realize that in the future, it will be companies such as AOL Time Warner that are likely to be the standard—companies that are built around the Net and infused by it, but that are not exclusive to it. The walls are coming down.

CHAPTER THREE

From C to Shining C

*The Consumer Internet:
Content, Commerce,
and Community*

I F YOU'RE LIKE a lot of people, you've probably used the Internet to do research, make travel arrangements, or shop for gifts. It's addictive, isn't it? You can click your mouse a few times, hop from site to site, comparison shop, and find twenty different versions of whatever it is you're looking for. And then, *ba da bing,* in a few seconds you've ordered it, and odds are it'll be at your house within a couple of days. It's almost too easy to spend money on-line. I'll never forget the time my father discovered the joys of Internet shopping. I found out when I came home and found a couple of boxes waiting for me. The next day, there were a couple more. And two days after that, a few more. Turns out he couldn't tear himself away. And he kept at it for a few weeks, until the novelty wore off—and the credit card bill came.

But for all the pleasures of the Net, have you ever thought about why it's so great? Sure, it's convenient. Sure, it's cheap. But why is it those things? What allows Internet stores to charge lower prices than their counterparts at the shopping mall? What about the Net makes it fundamentally different from earlier communication tools such as the telephone, radio, or television? The answers to these questions aren't as obvious as they seem. And before you rush off to invest your hard-earned dollars in Amazon.com, Yahoo!, or any other site you happen to like, you should have a basic understanding of how and why these sites work, as well as how they hope to make money.

What's All the Fuss About?

First, some fundamentals. As a communication tool, the Internet is different in two key ways from its predecessors:

1. Unlike the telephone, which allows for interactive, one-to-one communication between people in two locations, and unlike television, which allows for the one-way distribution of information from one point to many points, the Internet permits simultaneous, interactive communication among many points. Instead of a one-to-one medium or a one-to-many medium, the Net is a many-to-many medium. In that regard, it almost resembles shortwave radio—which allows people in many locations to communicate with one another—except that it's far more sophisticated. This may seem obvious, but it's a key reason the Net has opened up new business opportunities that the telephone and television never could.

2. Communication on the Internet can happen in real time, but it doesn't have to. The Net allows information to be stored and called up at any time, and it allows that information to be sorted in millions of different ways. Imagine a disorganized jumble of index cards, each containing information on some topic. Now imagine being able to sort those cards instantly, according to subject. The Internet is a lot like a giant jumble of billions of virtual index cards—Web pages, in Internet-speak—each filled with information. Programs called search engines help sort through the clutter and find the most pertinent information by subject matter or keywords. Again, this may seem obvious, but it is fundamental to why the Net is breaking new ground as a venue for running a business.

So the Net allows for interactive communication among many people in many locations, and it allows for a lot of information to be stored, retrieved, and sorted at any time. Why does this make for a whole new array of business opportunities? Let's start by thinking about the business I'm in: news. In the old days, finding out what was going on in the news meant getting a copy of a newspaper and finding an interesting article, or flipping on the TV and hoping you hadn't missed the big story. Now think about the news business in the age of the Internet. On the Net, users can quickly conduct research or obtain reams of news or data on virtually any topic—simply by entering a keyword or going to their favorite news site at any time of the day or night. Articles I write in the paper and interviews I conduct on television are archived on the Net and available anytime you want to look for them (go ahead, look!)—so that if you missed them the first time around, they're there for you to look at again, at your convenience. The Internet, in a nutshell, is the ultimate tool for information distribution and information gathering, because it provides a direct twenty-four-hour-a-day connection between the folks who have the information and the folks who want it.

For the same reason, the Net is also the ultimate shopping tool. Sellers can display an infinite catalog of goods to a huge community of potential buyers—you, me, my father—and it's available for us to look at—and buy—anytime we want. The same goes for communication. The Net is pretty much the only communication tool that permits simultaneous communication, both real-time and delayed, among large numbers of people, making it possible to create entire "virtual" communities where no communities existed before.

Against this backdrop, it's not surprising that Web businesses have evolved around three themes: content, commerce, and community (those in the know call them "the three C's," but it's just as easy to think of them as reading, shopping, and chatting). In the early days of the Web, a lot of companies chose to focus on just one of these themes. News sites were basically about providing news and information, the assumption being that they'd make money selling subscriptions or selling ads. Commerce sites sprang up just to sell things—you name it, there's probably a Web site that sells it. And community sites developed for the sole purpose of bringing together lots of people with similar interests.

It didn't take long, though, before a lightbulb clicked on and Web entrepreneurs realized there was no real reason they should be limited to doing business in just one category. Just as Barnes & Noble figured out it could sell a lot more books if it could keep people in its stores longer—and it could keep them in its stores longer if it sold them coffee and gave them a comfortable place to sit down and drink it—a lot of Internet commerce sites have found that building a community feeling among their shoppers helps create customer loyalty. So while eBay, for example, is mostly about buying and selling, it also offers discussion groups that aren't really about making money as much as they're about creating a sense of belonging among buyers and sellers. In the same way, many community sites have found that offering a few products for sale doesn't really take away from their community feel—and it's a pretty good way to earn some cold, hard cash. And many news sites now feature user chats about the day's headlines, as well as the occasional item for sale. After all, if you have folks on your site anyway, why not try to sell them something? As a result, the lines between the different categories have blurred substantially.

Point, Click, Shop!

Americans are consummate shoppers. As a nation, we have one of the world's lowest savings rates, and we account for a disproportionate share of consumption. We love to eat out, order in, hang out at the mall, and shop till we drop. We live to buy: clothes, shoes, jewelry, TVs, boom boxes, CDs, cars. And we crave convenience. Where else would it make sense for a catalog apparel retailer such as J. Crew to keep its phone lines open and ready to take orders twenty-four hours a day, seven days a week, 364 days a year?

Against this backdrop, it's hardly surprising that shopping was the function that, as much as any other, popularized the Internet as a mass-market phenomenon. Amazon's Jeff Bezos was one of the first to recognize and act on the new medium's potential as a consumer tool, quitting his job and trekking across the country to set up a Web site that aims to sell you anything you'll ever want to buy, all without leaving the comfort of your own home. (A Company Snapshot of Amazon's business follows.) Other entrepreneurs were quick to follow in Bezos's footsteps, setting up hundreds of on-line destinations offering everything from deodorant to golf balls to flea and tick repellent. (At one time, in early 2000, there were no fewer than four major pet supply sites, all established within about nine months of one another, as well as dozens of smaller sites. Not surprisingly, it didn't take long for many of these companies to go out of business!)

Company Snapshot: Amazon.com

At a Glance
Ticker symbol: AMZN
Founded: 1995
Went public: 1997
2000 revenue: $2.76 billion
Revenue growth rate (vs. 1999): 68%
2000 losses: $417 million
Profit growth rate (vs. 1999): NA
Key management: Jeff Bezos, President and Chief Executive Officer

Described by its own founder and chief executive as "famously unprofitable," Amazon.com is the biggest and best-known on-line retailer in the world. It is also, by some accounts, one of the greatest gambles in business history—a company that has, in its first half decade of existence, consumed billions of investor dollars and turned not a dime in profit. Ask founder Jeff Bezos, though, and he'll tell you he's convinced that Amazon will eventually become one of the world's most profitable companies. (Bezos promised in early 2001 that the company would turn a quarterly profit by the end of the year.)

Amazon's stated mission is deceptively simple: to become the one place anyone ever has to go on-line to buy just about anything. Bezos started out selling books, because there are so many books in the world that no one bookstore can hope to stock all, or even most, titles in any one shop—and because books are easy to describe in a catalog, easy to store in a warehouse, and easy to ship. Books thus seemed ideally suited to on-line commerce. But Amazon quickly branched out into other categories: compact discs, videos, toys, hardware, consumer electronics, cooking supplies, and lawn furniture among them. The company has also tried, less successfully, to compete with eBay in the auction arena, and its zShops category allows anyone to set up an on-line store, linked to Amazon, for a relatively modest fee.

Amazon's business model makes intuitive sense: by stockpiling its inventory in a few giant warehouses built on cheap land—rather than in hundreds of stores in high-rent districts all around the world—the company saves on real estate, inventory, and sales costs. It doesn't need to stock every item for sale in every store. And it doesn't need to pay salespeople to operate those stores. But make no mistake: Amazon's business is still very much rooted in the physical world. It owns millions of square feet of warehouse space, piled high with millions of dollars' worth of physical inventory. For most of that inventory, Amazon assumes the risk that if it doesn't sell, the company will be stuck with it.

In mid-2000, Amazon shifted gears, teaming up with Toys "R" Us to sell toys and children's products. Under the plan, Amazon handles the companies' joint Web site, as well as distribution. But Toys "R" Us orders most of the toys and assumes most of the inventory risk. Toys "R" Us pays Amazon a fee for its services, as well as a single-digit percentage of revenues. The arrangement reduces Amazon's toy-related revenues, but it also limits the company's potential losses, meaning that more of each dollar the company takes in will fall to the bottom line. The arrangement is particularly well suited to the toy business, which involves more inventory risk, concentrated into one all-important selling season (the holidays), than just about any other category. Still, Amazon is likely to seek out similar joint ventures in other categories as well, in an effort to reduce its inventory risk while improving its profitability.

Ultimately, analysts say, Amazon could exit the inventory business entirely, perhaps even splitting its business into two separate companies: a Web site that serves as a central destination for on-line commerce and a distribution business that handles shipping and handling for a host of different merchants. But such a transition isn't likely for some time. In the meantime, Amazon must convince investors that it can make meaningful and sustained profits doing what it's doing. And it faces a number of risks, including rivals that are attacking it from all sides. In addition, some analysts suggest that the company has yet to convince enough consumers that it's more than just a bookstore—something it's going to have to do if it's ever going to grow into its massive market capitalization.

According to Forrester Research, on-line consumer commerce in the United States totaled $8 billion in 1998, a number Forrester predicts will rise to $108 billion by the year 2003. So far, the products that have sold best on-line are airline tickets, books, music, computers, electronics, and clothes. Not surprisingly, those are things that shoppers don't feel a particular need to touch or feel before they buy. They're commodity-type items, not one-of-a-kinds. And, generally speaking, they're not major household purchases, where buyers are putting a lot at stake. That's one reason airline tickets and books have sold so well but jewelry and furniture haven't. Those items may catch on as the Web grows more popular and people get more comfortable with it, but my guess is that they'll always sell better off-line than on.

Why is the Internet so perfect for shopping? For one thing, it's spectacularly convenient. You can shop entirely on your own terms—whenever you want, wherever you want, wearing whatever you want—while avoiding crowds, lines, and pushy salespeople. There are no heavy bags to carry; items are delivered to your door within a few days, and occasionally even a few hours. And for the time being, unless Congress changes its mind—there's no sales tax on most on-line purchases, provided they're made from stores headquartered in a state other than your own. (Most states have a "use tax" on out-of-state purchases, but it's essentially unenforced.)

The Net is tailor-made for comparison shopping, making it possible to find the store offering the best price with just a few mouse clicks. Unlike traditional stores or catalogs, the Net is customizable. Many sites allow you to enter your own shopping pa-rameters—your likes, dislikes, and price ranges—and then offer you only the kinds of items you've specified. Search functions make it possible to search an entire store—or the entire Web—simply by entering the name of the item you're looking for.

OK, It's Convenient. So What?

It's easy to see why this convenience is great for you and me as consumers. But why should it matter to us as investors? Quite simply, if the Net is a great place to shop, people will shop there. And if people shop there, chances are somebody's going to figure out how to make money selling them things. As legendary investor Peter Lynch says, "I talk to hundreds of companies a year and spend hour after hour in heady powwows with CEOs, financial analysts, and my colleagues in the mutual fund business, but I stumble onto the big winners in extracurricular situations, the same way you could." Translation? The best investments are right under your nose. And the way to find them is, first and foremost, by paying attention to which on-line stores you and your friends frequent.

Aside from the benefits it offers consumers, the Net also offers a host of benefits to retailers that make it a potentially far more profitable way of doing business than the traditional way. Take overhead, for instance. Think of the Net as a catalog with infinite pages, a store with unlimited shelf space. Traditional stores have to display their goods for customers to see, absorbing the cost of the physical display space as part of their overhead. That's not cheap. In 1999, the average rent for retail space in a U.S. shopping mall was $22 per square foot per year. In New York City, rents averaged closer to $77 per square foot. That's before paying for heat, electricity, water, insurance, and repairs, not to mention the staff to run the store! Plus, there's inventory risk. After all, to operate a chain of stores across the country, you have to stock each one with merchandise.

A Preppy Example

Let's take J. Crew as an example. If it decides to sell a Nordic anorak this season, it has to stock several dozen Nordic anoraks at each of its stores in Mission Viejo, Sacramento, Santa Monica, Pasadena, and so on—and that's just California! Now multiply that by the eighty-one stores J. Crew has across the country. The Nordic anorak had better sell well, because in order to stock just a few dozen of them at each of its stores, J. Crew needs to buy several thousand. If they bomb, the company is going to be stuck with a lot of Nordic anoraks.

Catalog retailers have it a bit better, because their warehouses for storing goods don't have to be located in high-traffic (read: high-rent) districts, they don't have to operate as many of them (one distribution center can serve a huge area), and, with fewer physical locations, they don't have to hire as many salespeople. In addition, their inventory risk is lower. To sell that same Nordic anorak by mail, J. Crew needs to stock just one location—its Lynchburg, Virginia, distribution center—reordering more anoraks as they sell out. If the anorak doesn't sell, the company is stuck with a lot fewer duds.

At the same time, J. Crew still has a lot at stake with that anorak because it's taking up space in the company's catalog, and catalog space is limited. There are only so many pages consumers will read, and there is only so much that can be displayed on a single page. Plus, printing and mailing a catalog aren't free. The average 160-page catalog costs roughly $1 to print and ship, per copy. Multiply that by the 80 million catalogs J. Crew mails out each year, and that's an annual investment of $80 million *before* the company has sold a single item.

Now consider J. Crew's Web site: jcrew.com. It benefits from the same inventory and physical overhead advantages as the J. Crew catalog, but it doesn't have the same costs for printing and shipping. Building a retailing Web site, according to Forrester Research, costs anywhere from $2 million to $41 million, depending on how elaborate the site is and how much traffic it's designed to handle. But the virtual display space of the Internet is constrained only by the cost and availability of the computer memory needed to store the list of items for sale. And that's basically cheap and limitless. As a result, jcrew.com can, in theory at least, offer many more items for sale on-line than it can by mail or in its stores, and all at significantly lower cost to the company.

There's another advantage as well, one that only the Internet makes possible. Once J. Crew creates a display in its physical stores or prints its catalogs, it has pretty much bet the ranch on the items it has chosen to feature most prominently. Store displays are cumbersome to change, and once a catalog is printed, it can't be changed. If the Nordic anorak is featured on the cover of the Winter edition and it turns out not to be very popular, that cover is wasted. On the Web, though, it's no big deal to rejigger a display at a moment's notice, and at hardly any cost. Companies can also track what their customers are buying in real time. That means that if the anorak isn't selling well, it can be dumped instantly and replaced with something else—perhaps a hooded parka. And if the parka sells out, no problem: it, too, can be dumped in favor of something else.

Company Snapshot: barnesandnoble.com

At a Glance
Ticker symbol: BNBN
Founded: 1997
Went public: 1999
2000 revenue: $320.1 million
Revenue growth rate (vs. 1999): 65%
2000 losses: $158.2 million
Profit growth rate (vs. 1999): NA
Key management: Stephen Riggio, Chief Executive Officer

One of the few publicly traded Internet companies majority-owned by a bricks-and-mortar parent, barnesandnoble.com is, not surprisingly, the on-line bookselling arm of Barnes & Noble. In addition to books, the site also sells music, videos, and posters.

Established in the wake of Amazon.com, barnesandnoble.com has struggled to catch up to its Internet-only rival in total sales, despite its head start in developing brand awareness. But by many accounts, Barnes & Noble has a significant long-term advantage over rivals such as Amazon, in that its large land-based presence should help it keep marketing costs relatively low. Barnes & Noble has also been a leader in rolling out new initiatives such as e-books and same-day delivery, which it offers in parts of New York City.

Like other category-specific on-line retailers, the question confronting barnesandnoble.com is whether there is a big enough business selling mostly books on-line, given the low profit margins and significant investments in infrastructure and marketing such a business entails. Working in its favor is the fact that, as Amazon has already demonstrated, books are a category ideally suited to on-line sales. The Internet works well for cataloging and describing the hundreds of thousands of titles available for sale, books are easy to warehouse and ship, and customers don't generally feel the need to examine them up close before buying them. As a result, it's quite possible to sell books on-line profitably. Again, the key issue is how big a business on-line book retailing will ultimately become—and how big a market capitalization that implies for the company.

For investors, barnesandnoble.com has one added benefit. Though the stock has been, in its early years, one of the less exciting performers among the dot-com companies, barnesandnoble.com is unlikely ever to go out of business—a claim other Internet retailers cannot yet make. Even in a worst-case scenario, barnesandnoble.com is likely to be reabsorbed by its bricks-and-mortar parent before it is allowed to go under.

One caveat is that luring customers to the Web costs money, which diminishes some of the efficiency of operating on-line. Studies have shown, for example, that Web sites operating alongside catalogs yield more sales than Web sites operating on their own. (This is one reason some Net retailers have expanded into the catalog business.) On the other hand, once customers have shopped on-line, the Net offers an easy way to coax them back without printing another expensive catalog—or chasing them down the street after they've left a physical store. It's called e-mail. E-mail allows on-line stores to maintain a continuous, low-cost relationship with their shoppers, updating them about new items and specials or alerting them when desired items become available.

I Feel a Big "But" Coming

So far, so good. What's the downside, you ask? Obviously, there are drawbacks to operating a retail business on-line that don't exist off-line. For one thing, customers can't touch and feel the merchandise. There are no salespeople to offer advice—or to subtly pressure customers into buying. The simplicity of comparison shopping—and the fact that no store is more than a few mouse clicks away from its competition—means that it's difficult for stores to have any pricing power. And if setting up a Web site is a lot cheaper than opening a physical store, the flip side is that just about anybody can do so. Not everyone will succeed, of course, but the sheer number of Web stores constantly opening means that there's probably always more than one site offering identical goods at different prices. And with all those retail sites popping up, how can any single on-line retailer distinguish itself in customers' minds?

Successful Internet retailers have responded to these dilemmas by resorting to the two tactics that have kept many bricks-and-mortar retailers alive for years: branding and customer service. Beginning in mid-1999, on-line merchants flush with millions of newly raised investor dollars began pouring that money into flashy, expensive ad campaigns. In some cities, it became difficult to walk down a major street without being practically assaulted by (often annoying) ads for every form of dot-com company on buses, taxis, and telephone booths. For a time, major TV networks were rolling in Internet-related ad dollars. More than a dozen of the thirty or so companies advertising on the 2000 Super Bowl were dot coms, which coughed up roughly $2 million per thirty-second spot. (So great was the demand that ABC insisted on being paid in advance by several of the sketchier firms.)

This trend has diminished considerably since many dot coms began running out of cash—and investors became more wary of throwing new money at them. (Just three dot coms advertised on the 2001 Super Bowl.) Still, branding remains a mania among Internet firms. And who can blame them? The companies have a limited amount of time to prove to investors that they can attract customers and sell goods. So they turn around and dump dollars on ads, aiming to build the highest possible profile as quickly as possible. And the more a few companies advertise, the more every company has to advertise. At the height of the mania, several of the dot coms that advertised on the Super Bowl spent the bulk of their cash on those spots. Among them: computer.com, which offered information and support for novice computer users and buyers of computer-related products. It spent $3 million of the $5.8 million it raised from venture capital investors on Super Bowl ads. Sure enough, the Web site did see a surge in traffic in the days following the ads' appearance. But only 40,000 of those visitors turned into customers, not enough to sustain a business. Computer.com shut down its operations and sold its assets to another firm in early 2001. (In any case, I'd have a hard time putting my money behind a management team that's prepared to gamble the company's future on a couple of thirty-second TV spots.)

Those in favor of the mad dash to build brand argue that it does help build customer loyalty—and they're probably not entirely wrong. After all, why do so many of us pay more for Robitussen, when we know we could get generic cough syrup cheaper? The makers of Robitussen have convinced us it's worth the extra money—that it's safer, more effective, and more reliable. It's no different for Internet retailers. Why shop for a book at Amazon over barnesandnoble.com? Because that's the name that springs first to mind when you think "books" and "on-line." Why pay more at either site when you could buy the same book cheaper someplace else? Because Amazon and Barnes & Noble have convinced you that they'll get it to you faster, with less likelihood of a mix-up—and that their customer service staffs will be friendlier and more helpful if something goes wrong.

Customer service is the other area that many Internet retailers are counting on for survival, and they're spending heavily to get it right. Remember the argument about on-line retailing eliminating the overhead associated with stores and salespeople? Well, here's another big "but": customers, it turns out, are still pretty skeptical of on-line shopping. You and I might not be, but a lot of folks still think the added convenience of ordering Christmas gifts in their underwear is outweighed by the inconvenience of slow delivery and possibly mishandled orders. (A colleague of mine is a prime example. He ordered a "My First Hanukkah" T-shirt from eToys as a gift for a friend's new baby. What arrived, unfortunately, was a "My First Christmas" T-shirt. He called the company. "Our apologies," they said. "We'll ship another out right away." And they did. Within days, the friend's baby received another "My First Christmas" T-shirt.)

Company Snapshot: buy.com

At a Glance
Ticker symbol: BUYX
Founded: 1997
Went public: 2000
2000 revenue: $787.7 million
Revenue growth rate (vs. 1999): 32%
2000 losses: $97.7 million
Profit growth rate (vs. 1999): NA
Key management: Donald Kendall, Chairman, James Roszak, CEO

Like Amazon.com, buy.com aims to be an on-line superstore, though it focuses much more intently on electronics. And like Amazon, buy.com has, to date, not earned a dime. Beyond that, though, the two companies have very different business models. Buy.com owns no warehouses and stockpiles no inventory of its own. In addition, the company competes intensively on price. While Amazon believes its brand name allows it to command something of a price premium relative to other on-line merchants, buy.com is premised on the notion that it can be a low-price leader, thanks to its low cost structure, and that it can make money by selling goods in large volume.

Buy.com's virtual model stems in part from its tight relationship with the privately held Ingram distribution empire, one of the world's biggest stockpilers and distributors of books, electronics, and other merchandise for retailers. Ingram owns a significant stake in buy.com and maintains a seat on the buy.com board. In addition, Ingram handles the bulk of buy.com's inventory management and distribution. Orders placed on the buy.com Web site are, for the most part, routed to Ingram, which packs and ships the goods directly to the customer. This relationship allows buy.com to avoid both inventory risk and the massive investment required to build and run a big distribution operation. By the same token, it provides significant new business to Ingram without its having to assume the risk of building a big Internet operation on its own balance sheet or under its own brand—and without upsetting Ingram's own retail clients who might be upset if Ingram were competing directly with them as a retailer.

The risk is that by competing on price, buy.com may never be able to develop a meaningful profit margin. And if it strays from its pricing strategy, it risks alienating those customers who are particularly price-sensitive. What's more, by farming out inventory and distribution to a third party, the company loses direct control over its customer relationships. Whereas Amazon, for example, has earned consistently high marks for first-rate customer service—at the expense of its bottom line—buy.com has earned consistently lower marks, though its record has improved.

The answer, according to many Internet retailers, is premium service. For some firms, this means simply upgrading shipping methods without charging customers the incremental cost. Bill customers for standard mail delivery, the thinking goes, then "delight" them by shipping the merchandise overnight. ("Delighting" customers has become a favorite catchphrase among e-tailing executives.) Sure, such customer retention techniques are expensive, but the hope is that they'll pay off in the form of a loyal customer base.

"C" Stands for "Convergence"

Amazon.com has taken this logic a big step further by building half a dozen massive distribution centers across the United States—a total of more than 3 million square feet of warehouse space—in addition to several more internationally. These centers are stocked with hundreds of millions of dollars worth of inventory that Amazon has available for sale. Doesn't this fly in the face of the virtual business model on which Amazon was founded, the one that forecast fatter profits based on a lack of inventory and physical distribution costs? Sure. But bringing distribution in-house allows the company to maintain more control over its customer relationships. Outsourcing a book order to some third-party distributor reduces inventory risk and distribution cost, but it increases the risk that the order may be lost or improperly filled, and it limits Amazon's ability to do anything about the problem.

The thinking is that for a company to spend millions of dollars on advertising to woo customers, only to disappoint them once they show up, is a recipe for disaster. That's especially true when a lot of those customers don't really trust the Internet yet in the first place. If their very first order gets botched, they're likely never to come back. So Amazon and the firms copying its model are spending more up front on better customer service, in the hope that they'll keep a lot more of the customers who try them out. And, as Jeff Bezos points out to anyone who'll listen, owning half a dozen giant distribution centers is still a lot cheaper than building a chain of stores coast to coast and stocking each one. (Of course, not every management team accepts that notion. Buy.com, for example, outsources all its distribution, and it holds no inventory. Its customer satisfaction ratings are also consistently lower than Amazon's, though they are improving. And even Amazon has been forced to acknowledge that it overbuilt. It shut one of its distribution centers in early 2001, and said it would keep another open only during the holiday season.)

All this comes as bricks-and-mortar stores are flocking to the Internet. So far, none of them has been stunningly successful, though only a few have really tried very hard. Part of the problem is that most traditional retailers were late to the game because they didn't take the Internet seriously at first. Now they're playing catch-up. As a result, the Web sites they've designed have generally been clumsy, and they haven't been well promoted.

Let's take a prominent example, Toysrus.com. Launched in June 1998, Toysrus.com came to market with a well-known brand name and a network of real-world stores and supplier relationships. The company also teamed up with Benchmark Capital, the venture capital firm that first funded eBay, to develop its on-line business. From the start, though, Toysrus.com was plagued by management difficulties and mistakes. The Benchmark relationship broke down over control issues. The company's brand name succeeded in bringing customers to the Web site—but was tarnished when the site crashed several times during the height of the 1999 holiday shopping season. And during that season, Toysrus.com continually ran out of popular items or botched orders, alienating thousands of new customers. In its first year, Toys "R" Us's on-line sales totaled just $49 million. Amazon's toy sales, meanwhile, topped $95 million in the fourth quarter alone, even though it had launched its toy division only a few months before the season began. (More recently, Amazon and Toys "R" Us have combined their on-line toy-selling operations with Toys "R" Us handling the purchasing of toys and Amazon handling both Web site management and the warehousing and distribution of those toys. The deal allows Amazon to concentrate on the areas it knows best—Internet operations and customer service—while avoiding the area it has least expertise in and that carries the most risk—inventory management. Similarly, for Toys "R" Us, the deal was a face-saving way of exiting from its own unsuccessful Internet venture while maintaining an Internet presence.)

For all their early blunders, though, you shouldn't count traditional retailers out. Many have teamed up with Web-savvy venture capitalists to launch separate Internet divisions. Wal-Mart and Kmart are good examples. For a long time, Wal-Mart's dot-com division didn't make a dent against Amazon in terms of the total quantity of goods sold on-line, suffering from a badly designed Web site that the company barely advertised and that offered products different from what Wal-Mart had for sale in its stores. But the division has gained momentum ever since Wal-Mart spun it off as a separate company, partly owned by Accel Partners, a Silicon Valley venture capital firm, and brought in new leadership. Kmart did something similar, partnering with Softbank and with Yahoo! to launch its own separately branded site, BlueLight.com. These sites potentially offer the best of both worlds: already established brand names and real-world stores customers can visit to return or exchange products, combined with Net-savvy leadership.

The bottom line? Traditional retailers are starting to look a lot more like their upstart dot-com rivals, even as dot-com retailers are starting to look more like traditional retailers, with bricks-and-mortar infrastructures and massive inventories. In Internet-speak, that's called convergence. For investors like you and me, that might suggest a sea of undifferentiated clones, with one investment opportunity looking pretty much identical to the next. In reality, though, it means just the opposite: *more* choices. Conservative investors might opt for a real-world store with a dot-com division—say, a Wal-Mart or Kmart—that probably isn't a particularly risky play but may not be fantastically rewarding in the short term, either. More aggressive investors might want to juice up their portfolios with a riskier bet on an Amazon.com. And really gutsy types might want to take their chances on a truly virtual company, such as buy.com, that may soar—but may just as easily crash and burn.

All the News That's Fit to Download

So much for commerce. Let's turn now to one of the other "Cs," content. Even before the Net turned into the first global shopping mall, it was the first global public library (thankfully, without the overdue fees!)—an archive for storing endless reams of information on just about every topic imaginable. Years before Amazon was a sparkle in Jeff Bezos's eye, the Net was used at colleges and universities, allowing students and scholars to communicate with one another and to post information for broader viewing. As recently as 1996, according to Jupiter Media Metrix, the ten most popular sites on the Web belonged to universities. (Today, the top ten are all for-profit commerce, content, or community sites of one form or another.) Eventually, though, the notion spread beyond the ivory tower. Private, computerized legal databases such as Lexis-Nexis migrated to the Web, where they were accessible to any lawyer with an Internet connection. Scientific databases, such as MED-LINE, made the move as well, as did financial organizations from banks and brokerages to news and data companies such as Dow Jones, Reuters, and Bloomberg.

Many of these early Web efforts weren't designed to make money. Others were targeted at a limited audience—doctors, lawyers, traders—who would pay to access the information. Eventually, though, as the Net grew more popular, entrepreneurs began to see much greater profit potential. Newspapers and magazines began experimenting with posting some stories on-line and charging for advertising (early on, most were afraid to put too many stories on-line because they thought readers would stop buying the print editions). *The Wall Street Journal* began charging a fee to subscribe to its online version. And then came the first Internet-only publications: magazines such as Slate and Salon.com, financial news sites such as MarketWatch.com and TheStreet.com, technology sites such as CNET.com and general news sites such as CNN.com and MSNBC (the last two in partnership with TV news operations but focused mostly on content created just for the Web). Other sites—including Yahoo! and many of the other search engines, such as Lycos—began pulling together and organizing various content offerings under one roof. These sites became known as "portals" because they provided gateways to all sorts of information available online.

Most of these companies offered their content free of charge, hoping to make money the same way TV and radio stations make money: advertising. In fact, because the Internet was in theory so cheap to produce—no studios to maintain, no expensive talent to pay, no newsprint to buy—its profit margins could be fatter.

It Sounded Like a Great Idea . . .

But what works in theory doesn't always work in practice. Most of the sites that did try charging subscription fees found that people weren't subscribing because other sites offered similar content for free. On TV, viewers may choose to watch Tom Brokaw instead of Dan Rather because they like Brokaw's personality better. But on the Net, a stock price on MarketWatch.com is identical to the stock price on TheStreet.com. In fact, there are dozens of sites that can give you an instant stock quote or tell you what the weather's like in Boston or what's going on in Bosnia, so their content is a commodity that few people are willing to pay to see.

One exception is my own publication, *The Wall Street Journal,* which has been able to develop a paying audience of several hundred thousand members without cannibalizing its print editions. But the *Journal* is probably the exception that proves the rule. Its content is time-sensitive, specialized, and available nowhere else. Only one site carries the *Journal*'s brand name and its reputation for breaking important business news on a regular basis, and people have been willing to pay for those. (End of shameless self-promotion!)

By and large, though, even high-quality content doesn't always make for a high-quality business. As magazines go, for example, Salon is generally perceived to be well written and provocative. But people have only so much time to read, on-line or off. To win an audience, Salon has to compete with every other magazine, many of which have loyal followings. As a result, Salon's audience has remained pretty small, and as an investment, it's been a dog.

The lesson? Don't invest in a content company simply because it offers good content. Just as selling top-flight merchandise is an indicator, but not a guarantee, that a retailer will succeed, offering top-flight news or information is an indicator, but not a guarantee, that a content company will make money. TheStreet.com and Salon are both prominent examples of sites that have high quality content but haven't been able to develop a wide enough audience to support them.

Just like Web retailers, Web content companies have poured

money into advertising and marketing in an attempt to build a brand name and an audience. Some, such as MarketWatch, have tried to conserve cash by swapping big chunks of themselves for advertising time (MarketWatch traded CBS a 38 percent stake in itself, along with a share of its revenues, for $30 million worth of advertising over five years, as well as use of the CBS name, logo, and certain news content). The idea is simple: if you can't support yourself by charging your audience, try to get a big enough audience that advertisers will pay you to access it. It's essentially the same business model as in TV and radio. The difference is that all the TV and radio stations in the world don't come close to matching the number of Web sites trying to support themselves with advertising. And those stations didn't all just spring up at once; it took years for them to develop, giving the TV and radio advertising market time to develop. Web advertising hasn't matured yet, but there are hundreds of Web sites that are counting on advertising to keep them alive. With so many sites competing for a limited number of ad dollars, there's simply not enough money to go around.

So far, only a handful of sites with the biggest audiences—including Yahoo! and Lycos—have been able to make any real money on ad sales. The bad news: most sites don't have a prayer of supporting themselves long-term on advertising alone. Many sites will go out of business or be acquired; some already have. The good news: companies are learning that advertising isn't the only answer. Many sites are supplementing ad revenue with other income by selling things to their customers. In addition, as more and more Web sites fall by the wayside, they leave fewer and fewer survivors behind, making the competition for ad dollars that much less intense. It's survival of the fittest, at Internet speed. Meanwhile, Internet advertising is gradually becoming more popular, partly because it's becoming more effective. Companies have found that the Internet lets them target prospective customers better than almost any other medium. Potential customers can be followed from site to site, their interests and purchases can be tracked, and ads can be aimed right at them.

For the moment, though, Internet content sites make for very risky investments and are best tackled by those with lead-lined stomachs and an appetite for volatility. With few exceptions—such as Yahoo!—most Net content stocks have been duds, TheStreet.com, Salon.com, and NBCi among them. This isn't really surprising. Other than dot-com hype, so far most of these sites are little more than gussied-up magazines and newspapers presented on-line. There's an appeal to that concept. There's probably even an audience for a lot of it. But for the moment, there's not a lot of money in it.

So far, the Internet content sites that have been most successful are those, like *The Wall Street Journal*, CNN, and MSNBC, that are affiliated with real-world news organizations. These sites have been able to attract relatively big audiences without spending very much on advertising. That's partly due to their already powerful brand names and partly due to the fact that they are able to promote themselves on their existing media outlets. What's more, they're able to save money on the production side by recycling much of the content from the print or television side of their business for use on the Web. That means that most of what they earn drops straight to the bottom line. So far, so good. The problem for investors is that none of these sites, so far, is publicly traded on its own. While the *Journal*, *The New York Times*, and others have considered spinning off their Web businesses as separately traded stocks, they've shied away from doing that so far. If and when they do, they're likely to do so as tracking stocks, which carry their own drawbacks (among them that they don't actually confer ownership of the assets whose performance they're designed to track). Still, investors who are interested in getting a bit of Internet spark out of an otherwise conservative investment may want to put some dollars to work in these types of traditional media companies. They're not likely to double or triple overnight, but they're not likely to end up worthless either—and their on-line success may add a little sizzle to their performance.

As for the pure-play Net content companies, though, without the ability to charge subscription fees, these sites need to attract huge audiences to become profitable. Even Yahoo!, the most successful content site of all and the largest Internet site, is only modestly profitable when compared to companies outside the Internet that carry similar market values. And it's making a mad dash to branch out beyond content—seeking to build up its reputation as a virtual shopping mall and charging retailers "rent" to set up stores on its site, even as it helps big companies build their internal Web sites—in an effort to make sure its profitability will hold up over the long run. The bottom line: content is a nice attribute and advertising is a nice additional source of revenue for sites that also have other things going for them. But, with a few exceptions, neither one makes a great business by itself.

Company Snapshot: Yahoo!

At a Glance
Ticker symbol: YHOO
Founded: 1994
Went public: 1996
2000 revenue: $1.1 billion
Revenue growth rate (vs. 1999): 88%
2000 profits: $291 million
Profit growth rate (vs. 1999): 111%
Key management: Tim Koogle, Chairman and Chief Executive Officer

Yahoo was founded by a couple of Stanford University graduate students—Jerry Yang and David Filo—who wanted to create a directory of the best and most popular Web sites. Seeking to emphasize their easygoing, antibureaucratic style, they named their company Yahoo!, short for Yet Another Hierarchical Officious Oracle. They called themselves the Chief Yahoos.

As Yahoo!'s popularity grew, Yang and Filo dropped out of Stanford to devote themselves full-time to their venture. It was a wise move. Today, the company is the world's leading Internet portal—and one of its largest companies—mentioned regularly as a potential merger partner for venerable media titans ranging from the Walt Disney Company to Rupert Murdoch's News Corporation. Yang and Filo are thirtysomething billionaires.

Yahoo!'s mission is, in short, to create a single Web site that brings together the best content available on the Web. It creates little of its own content, concentrating instead on amassing and integrating content created by others under their own brand names. Check out Yahoo!'s news pages, and you'll find news stories from Reuters, the Associated Press, and a host of newspapers from around the world. Check out its finance pages, and you'll find content from Bloomberg, TheStreet.com, and CBS MarketWatch.com. Yahoo! is deliberately agnostic, believing that the better, and more flexible business model is to distribute content, rather than to manufacture it.

The company is similarly agnostic when it comes to the distribution of its own content. Unlike America Online, which acquired Time Warner in part to acquire its huge stable of brand-name content and in part to acquire its massive cable infrastructure, with cable lines that can distribute that content into millions of homes, Yahoo! has repeatedly emphasized its desire to stay "technology agnostic"— available over cable, satellite, and traditional dial-up Internet services, but with no interest in actually owning any of those high-cost physical distribution infrastructures. The company's virtual business model allows it to stay both nimble and extremely profitable.

Yahoo!'s approach might seem simple to replicate—and many have tried, from Lycos to Disney (through its failed GO.com portal) to NBC (through its NBCi portal). None have come close to toppling this Web leader, though, for two reasons. First, Yahoo!'s first-mover advantage helped it establish a base of popularity that feeds on itself, and its near-flawless execution of its business model hasn't given others an opportunity to grab market share. Simply put, Yahoo! is the first place millions of people go when they log onto the Internet—and until now, no one has given them a reason to change that habit.

Yahoo! makes money mostly through advertising, and its advertising base includes many of the world's blue chip companies. Though its advertising revenues are clearly tied to the growth of the Internet as an advertising medium, this much is clear: for many companies that are going to advertise on-line, their first stop is Yahoo! More recently, Yahoo! has tried to diversify its revenue base away from advertising, setting up an on-line shopping mall where hundreds of merchants hawk their wares (Yahoo! takes a cut of their sales) and even helping companies set up and operate those sites for a fee. Yahoo! is also helping companies develop their own internal Web sites, with content from Yahoo!—a business many believe could be a major revenue driver as more and more companies set up such sites.

It Takes a (Global) Village . . .

Commerce companies use the Internet as a new outlet for the distribution of goods. Content sites use it to improve the distribution of information. But only community sites really use the Internet to accomplish something totally new: the creation of faceless "virtual" communities of individuals, where no such communities could have existed before. No other medium allows masses of people to come together anonymously, with only their interests in common. Enter any "chat room," and you'll find dozens, if not hundreds, of people talking about every topic imaginable, identified only by aliases. A now-famous cartoon from *The New Yorker* magazine reads, "On the Internet, no one knows you're a dog."

Clearly, there's an element of entertainment to Internet communities. In some ways, it's like having a pen pal—only better, because it's in real time. It's fun to log on and "chat" about any given subject with people who may be around the corner—but may also be around the world. In the hit movie *You've Got Mail,* two lovelorn singles who live a few blocks from each other meet on the Internet, eventually coming face to face and finding true romance. Though fictional, this story is completely plausible. Already there are countless examples of people meeting, and marrying, via the World Wide Web. Unfortunately, there are also stories of real-life danger arising out of what started as innocent chats with seemingly friendly strangers.

It's probably too soon to know whether this entertainment aspect of Internet communities will subside like so many other fads. But Internet chats can also be very practical, creating a worldwide community of advice givers, product testers, and problem solvers. Name any medical condition, and there's almost certainly an Internet community of those suffering from it—or their friends and relatives coping with it—offering support and advice. Name any kitchen appliance or computer accessory, and there are legions of Internet chatters offering warnings or testimonials about its quality. Name any practical problem—how to make a great soufflé, how to get oil stains out of the driveway, how to find a hot stock—and there are thousands of people all over the world ready to pass along a friendly tip to you, a total stranger.

These types of virtual communities couldn't have existed before the Internet. But how can you make a business out of them? Launching an Internet community is relatively cheap. It requires little up-front investment: there's no need to buy merchandise, or lease warehouses, and the content is mostly free because it's contributed by the members themselves. As with other Web businesses, advertising can be expensive. But community sites have a key feature that most commerce and content sites can only dream about: a snowball-like ability to become more useful, and more popular, because of how useful and popular they already are. In Internet-speak, this is called "virality," and it's the Holy Grail of every Internet company everywhere. The idea: that every user of a Web site can "infect" other, potential users, drawing them into the site. To some extent, a well-run retail site is viral, in that good experiences are likely to spread by old-fashioned word of mouth. But retailers don't generally become better at what they do simply because they have more customers. (A notable exception to this is an auction site like eBay, which does become a better place to shop, and to sell products, as more people use it to buy and sell goods.) Community sites, on the other hand, are the definition of viral: the bigger they get, the more vibrant and useful they are; the more vibrant and useful they are, the more likely they are to attract new members.

Community sites are also generally very "sticky." That means users spend a lot of time on the sites and come back frequently for return visits. Advertisers crave "stickiness," because it means more time spent looking at their ads. Community sites are usually sticky because, simply put, it takes time to carry on a conversation.

At the same time, while they're viral in theory, few existing community sites are very big. That's because Internet communities depend on people who—to put it bluntly—have a lot of time on their hands that they're prepared to fritter away at a keyboard, chatting with people they've never met and, in most cases, never will.

Despite these obstacles, a number of entrepreneurs have tried to create big Internet communities. One early success story was GeoCities, which was sold to Yahoo! in early 1999 for more than $4 billion in stock. The site provides users with free, easy-to-use tools for creating personal Web pages. It's sticky, and it's inherently viral: members tell their friends about their Web pages, and their friends are then likely to use GeoCities to create their own Web pages. That makes the site popular with advertisers—and that's what attracted Yahoo!. But while the merger was a win for GeoCities investors, it was a much more marginal success for Yahoo!'s investors. GeoCities did bring more user eyeballs to Yahoo!, and it increased the portal's stickiness. But it's not clear that those improvements were worth $4 billion.

Company Snapshot: eBay

At a Glance
Ticker symbol: EBAY
Founded: 1995
Went public: 1998
2000 revenue: $431.4 million
Revenue growth rate (vs. 1999): 92%
2000 profits: $58.6 million
Profit growth rate (vs. 1999): 220%
Key management: Meg Whitman, President and Chief Executive Officer

One of the biggest, and most consistently profitable of the on-line commerce sites, eBay got its start quite by accident, when founder Pierre Omidyar tried to figure out a way to use the Internet to sell Pez dispensers. His creation ended up becoming the world's most popular on-line auction site—indeed, one of the most popular Web sites, period—and it made Omidyar an overnight billionaire.

Like most great ideas, eBay's business model is remarkably simple: The site acts as a meeting place for buyers and sellers. Sellers put items up for sale, and buyers bid on them. eBay charges a modest listing fee, as well as a commission on every sale. The beauty of this "person-to-person" business model is that it requires a minimal investment to operate. eBay owns no inventory and handles no distribution. It simply facilitates sales between others.

No one could have predicted how popular eBay would become, but now millions of people the world over use the site to unload all sorts of tchatchkes they could otherwise never sell—and millions of other people shop there. What's more, though it started out as a flea market—with most of the items sold little more than cheap collectibles—eBay has quickly become a place to sell everything from valuable art and antiques to cars to real estate. The company acquired Butterfield and Butterfield, one of the nation's oldest traditional auction houses. And its management has been aggressive about building up the company's brand name, as well as pursuing new revenue opportunities that arise from its core business. Its Billpoint payment-processing unit facilitates credit card payments, allowing individual sellers on the site to accept credit card payments from individual buyers for a small fee. In mid-2000, eBay acquired Half.com, an upstart site that allows users to sell goods at fixed prices, so long as those prices are no more than half the items' original retail value. And eBay is also helping other companies develop auction sites of their own that are tied into eBay's central Web site. For example, eBay now powers a site for Disney that auctions off Disney paraphernalia.

eBay's business might seem easy to replicate, and others have tried, including both Amazon and Yahoo!. But eBay's first-mover advantage has proved impossible to overcome. Simply put, eBay's popularity drives its success. Users know that if they put items up for sale there, they'll attract more bids than on other on-line auction sites. That success drives more users to put more items up for sale there—and the expanded selection attracts more bidders. The cycle feeds on itself, allowing little possibility for rivals to encroach on eBay's turf. The company has had a bit more difficulty replicating this success overseas, particularly in Japan, where Yahoo! set up shop earlier and has enjoyed some of the first-mover advantage eBay enjoys in the United States. Still, eBay has become such a worldwide phenomenon that its success elsewhere is helping it close the gap even in Japan.

Meanwhile, for every GeoCities, there are dozens of sites that have been a lot less successful. One competing service, Tripod, was less popular and was ultimately sold to Lycos for a much smaller price. Another competitor, theglobe.com, managed to go public in a spectacular IPO, but saw its shares spiral downward almost immediately, and hasn't ever recovered. iVillage, a site aimed at women that blends original content with various community features, has also been a lousy investment. It faces a host of competitors, and has tried to attract users with an expensive advertising campaign, but it's still a long way from making any money. Other sites—most still privately held because investors' appetite for more community offerings has sagged—continue to tough it out, hoping their fortunes will improve. A number of sites from Silicon Investor to Raging Bull—both now part of larger portals—are aimed at investors and day traders. Others, such as MyFamily.com, offer users a chance to trace their family trees; still others, like Vault.com, offer employees an opportunity to vent anonymously about their employers. The list goes on and on.

For the most part, though, pure community sites have been money losers, and very few publicly traded companies are still targeting this niche alone. Most community sites now offer some original content to complement their "chat" offerings, and they provide commerce opportunities as well, offering users a chance to buy something while they're there. At the same time, other Internet companies are trying to incorporate aspects of community into their businesses in an effort to become stickier and more viral. That's why Yahoo! bought GeoCities, why eBay offers a "Coffee Shop" section for its members to post messages, why Raging Bull is now part of the Lycos portal, and why CNBC.com offers "message boards" for its users to interact on.

For investors, community sites are probably more of a lesson learned than a moneymaking opportunity. The lesson: that Internet businesses may work well in theory, but they don't always work in practice. On the one hand, virtual communities are possible only on the Net. And there are many intuitive reasons to think the community model makes financial sense: it's cheap to get up and running, it's viral, and it's sticky. As it happens, though, almost nobody has managed to create a successful business out of a community site. The upshot: it's probably smarter to look for other Internet investments—whether retailers or content providers—that offer community-like qualities but aren't built just for the sake of being communities.

Knee Deep in Numbers

So much for theory; what does all this look like in practice? Let's take a look at the income statements of three Web sites of different types to get an idea.

Check out Amazon's earnings report (read that: loss report) for the fourth quarter of 2000, the all-important Christmas shopping season, with comparisons from the previous year (see accompanying income statement). While accounting standards demand comparisons with year-ago figures, for Internet companies the more relevant comparisons are often to the preceding quarter. That's because the companies tend to grow so fast that they invariably show growth relative to the prior year, so that last year's comparisons frequently tell you very little. Sequential quarter comparisons, on the other hand, often provide a better look at how they're doing *right now*. It's also harder to hide bad news in sequential reports. For example, in the balance sheet section, there is a breakdown of Amazon's assets. Check out the cash line. It's more than $800 million, up from $133 million a year earlier. That looks great. But Amazon is losing money! How did it add $700 million to its bank account over the past year? One reason is that the company raised more than $600 million early in the year in a bond offering, which it said it would use to build more distribution centers in Europe. Indeed, if you look a little further down, at the long-term debt line, you'll see that Amazon now owes $2.1 billion, up from just under $1.5 billion the prior year. But the bond offering doesn't explain everything. If you looked at the prior quarter, you'd see that Amazon's cash totaled just $647 million—meaning it surged by close to $200 million over the past three months. What explains that? The answer is that Amazon users pay the company by credit card—so Amazon receives the money immediately—but Amazon pays its own bills more slowly. In this case, a look at the liabilities section of Amazon's report compared with the prior quarter indicates that the company's accounts payable and accrued expenses (both of which measure its

AMAZON.COM, INC.
Statements of Operations
(in thousands, except per share data)

| | THREE MONTHS ENDED DECEMBER 31, | |
	2000	1999
Net sales	$972,360	$676,042
Cost of sales	748,060	588,196
Gross profit	224,300	87,846
Operating expenses:		
Marketing sales, and fulfillment	186,223	179,424
Technology and content	69,791	57,720
General and administrative	28,232	26,051
Stock-based compensation	(1,112)	14,049
Amortization of goodwill and other intangibles	79,210	82,301
Impairment-related and other	184,052	2,085
Total operating expenses	546,396	361,630
Loss from operations	(322,096)	((273,784)
Interest income	10,979	8,972
Interest expense	(36,094)	(18,142)
Other income (expense), net	(5,365)	(366)
Non-cash investment gains and losses, net	(155,005)	—
Net interest expense and other	(185,485)	(9,536)
Loss before equity in losses of equity method investees	(507,581)	(283,320)
Equity in losses of equity method investees, net	(37,559)	(39,893)
Net loss	$(545,140)	$(323,213)
Basic and diluted loss per share	$(1.53)	$(0.96)
Shares used in computation of basic and diluted loss per share	355,681	338,389
Pro Forma Results		
Pro forma loss from operations	$(59,946)	$(175,349)
Pro forma net loss	(90,426)	(184,885)
Pro forma basic and diluted loss per share	(0.25)	(0.55)
Shares used in computation of pro forma basic and diluted loss per share	355,681	338,389

AMAZON.COM, INC.
Balance Sheets
(in thousands, except per share data)

	DECEMBER 31, 2000	DECEMBER 31, 1999
ASSETS		
Current assets:		
Cash and cash equivalents	$822,435	$133,309
Marketable securities	278,087	572,879
Inventories	174,563	220,646
Prepaid expenses and other current assets	86,044	79,643
Total current assets	1,361,129	1,006,477
Fixed assets, net	366,416	317,613
Goodwill, net	158,990	534,699
Other intangibles, net	96,335	195,445
Investments in equity method investees	52,073	226,727
Other investments	40,177	144,735
Other assets	60,049	40,154
Total assets	$2,135,169	$2,465,850
LIABILITIES		
Current liabilities:		
Accounts payable	$485,383	$463,026
Accrued expenses and other current liabilities	272,683	176,208
Unearned revenue	131,117	54,790
Interest payable	69,196	24,888
Current portion of long-term debt and other	16,577	14,322
Total current liabilities	974,956	733,234
Long-term debt	2,127,464	1,466,338

short-term debts) jumped by nearly $300 million over the previous three months. The conclusion? Amazon's available cash is close to $300 million less than what the cash line on its balance sheet seems to indicate. But that information would not have been obvious simply from reading the earnings release as the company presented it, with year-over-year comparisons.

That said, the standard for reporting earnings is to show comparisons relative to the prior year, so making sequential quarter comparisons requires you to do some extra legwork. If you're lazy and don't want to go that extra mile, you can make do with reports as the companies provide them to you, but you risk overlooking some significant trends.

In Amazon's case, a couple of things should leap out at you right away. First is that the company's net sales jumped by more than 40 percent over the prior year. This is good, although it's a slower rate of growth than in the prior year (when Amazon's sales nearly tripled). Now take a look at the gross profit line, which shows the difference between the retail price of the goods and what Amazon paid for them (but doesn't include the expenses of running the company). It more than doubled. If you divide gross profits by overall revenues, you come up with a figure called the "gross profit margin." Stated in percentage terms, it indicates how many pennies of profit the company earns on every dollar's worth of goods sold, before most expenses. But even without this additional math, it's easy to see that although Amazon is growing more slowly, it is making more money on each sale.

Next look at operating expenses. They jumped by more than 50 percent—significantly faster than the rate Amazon's sales increased. This is not good. If you care enough to look at the breakdown, you'll see that a big part of the jump came from non-cash losses on investments. These aren't a good thing, certainly, but they're not as important as the performance of Amazon's underlying operations. As far as those are concerned, Amazon spent the most money on sales and marketing. While it's not smart to rely too much on this number (Internet companies tend to throw everything but the kitchen sink into their sales and marketing expenses category), generally speaking, sales and marketing expenses are one of the more variable parts of a company's business. In other words, if it felt the need, Amazon could presumably cut these expenses way down, boosting the bottom line. And indeed, it makes sense that marketing expenses and fulfillment costs (the cost of picking and packing products for shipping) would increase during the critical holiday season.

One more point: At the bottom of Amazon's income statement, you'll notice a section detailing Pro Forma Results. These numbers look a lot better than the ones above, because they exclude most non-cash expenses, including those investment losses (most of which came from stakes Amazon had in other Internet companies). Amazon would rather have investors look at these numbers—and indeed, they're the ones most analysts use—though some would argue that they aren't the most accurate reflection of the company's health.

Of course, going by the numbers alone isn't a good idea. If you've got time, and it's available, listening to the analysts' conference call can be helpful, at least to give you a sense of whether Wall Street is reacting positively or negatively to the news. It's also helpful to read the text that accompanies the earnings numbers. Naturally, this is practically always positive and puts the best possible spin on the numbers. But occasionally there's something useful in it. In this case, Amazon's press release indicated that it expects to turn an operating profit for the first time in the fourth quarter of 2001, though it also considerably reduced Wall Street's sales expectations for the year.

All in all, judging from this quick scan of Amazon's earnings report, you'd have to give the company no more than a C or a C plus for the quarter. It improved its profit margins, and expects to turn profitable within a year, but its sales growth slowed dramatically, and is likely to slow still further. As an investment, Amazon isn't for the faint of heart or those with short time horizons. But there are reasons for gutsier investors to give it some serious thought.

Now let's turn to a big content-focused Web site, Yahoo!. A couple of things jump out immediately as very different from Amazon. First, check out the income from operations. That's right, there is some! In contrast to Amazon, Yahoo! actually made money in the quarter—and it made close to 60 percent more than it made the prior year (not counting those pesky investment losses). While

YAHOO! INC.
Consolidated Statements of Operations
(in thousands, except per share amounts)

| | THREE MONTHS ENDED DECEMBER 31, | |
	2000	1999
Net revenues	$310,873	$203,148
Cost of revenues	40,071	27,712
Amortization of purchased technology	2,243	2,291
Total cost of revenues	42,314	30,003
Gross profit	268,559	173,145
Operating expenses:		
Sales and marketing	122,252	66,970
Product development	29,179	19,836
General and administrative	17,974	11,637
Payroll taxes on option exercises	2,566	10,345
Stock compensation expense	3,708	5,515
Amortization of intangibles	5,418	3,676
Acquisition-related costs	—	(444)
Total operating expenses	181,097	117,535
Income from operations	87,462	55,610
Investment income (loss), net	(138,502)	10,852
Minority interests in operations of consolidated subsidiaries	124	(809)
Income (loss) before income taxes	(50,916)	65,653
Provision for income taxes	46,903	27,889
Net income (loss)	$(97,819)	$37,764
Net income (loss) per share—diluted	$(0.17)	$0.06
Shares used in per share calculation—diluted	559,872	609,136

YAHOO! INC.
Consolidated Summary Balance Sheet Data
(in thousands)

	December 31, 2000	December 31, 1999
ASSETS		
Cash, cash equivalents, and investments in marketable debt securities	$1,688,666	$1,004,301
Accounts receivable, net	90,561	56,454
Property and equipment, net	109,781	60,798
Investments in marketable equity securities	87,545	250,966
Other assets	293,023	147,610
Total assets	$2,269,576	$1,520,129
LIABILITIES		
Liabilities:		
Accounts payable	$26,040	$14,341
Accrued expenses and other liabilities	200,144	107,303
Deferred revenue	117,165	90,790
Total liabilities	343,349	212,434

the overall number is relatively small ($87 million, after all, isn't all that much money when you think about a company that investors are valuing in the many billions of dollars), it's definitely headed in the right direction—and quickly.

More significantly, Yahoo!'s revenues also jumped, to more than $300 million. The trend is good, and while the overall number is smaller than Amazon's, that's to be expected. Remember, Yahoo! isn't selling goods directly—it's mostly selling advertising. So you would expect its revenues (the "top line") to be smaller on a relative basis, but its expenses should also be relatively smaller. That means more revenues should drop to the bottom line in the form of profits—which is exactly what happened. In fact, while Yahoo!'s revenues increased by 53 percent, its operating income increased by 57 percent. Translation? Not only is Yahoo! selling more, but as its sales increase, a bigger chunk of each sale is falling to the bottom line. This is known as *leverage,* and it's a very good thing.

One last point about Yahoo!'s financial results: while you won't find it in the income statement, if you read Yahoo!'s press release, you'll find mention of the Web site's "traffic" as measured in "average daily page views." Essentially, this is a rough measure of how many people are looking at the site each day, keeping in mind that each user probably accounts for at least a few page views as he jumps around from one part of the site to the next. This number is particularly important for content and community sites, as it indicates how popular they are—and hence how valuable to advertisers (in Amazon's case, popularity is straightforward—it's documented in terms of customers and overall sales; that's not the case at a content or community site, where the company isn't actually selling anything). Yahoo!'s report indicates that page views nearly doubled from the prior year, to more than 900 million—again, a strong overall number and strong growth.

All in all, Yahoo!'s numbers indicate that it is a solidly profitable company, with a solid business model that suggests that it will become more profitable as its popularity continues to increase. The biggest negative in Yahoo!'s report is that its overall profitability remains small for a company with such a huge market value, and its earnings release includes a cautious outlook, due to concerns over a softening advertising market. Still, Yahoo!'s profits are growing, and quickly. It gets an A minus for the quarter, and it shows good signs of being a strong Internet play—riskier and more volatile, perhaps, than an investment in General Electric but less risky by far than an investment in Amazon.

Now let's take a look at a major community site: iVillage. First, note its overall revenues. The number is tiny—less than $20 million—and it grew by little more than 11 percent over the prior year. Remember, Yahoo! *earned* more than four and a half times that amount in the same quarter, and its revenues jumped by more than 50 percent!

iVILLAGE, INC., AND SUBSIDIARIES
Condensed Consolidated Statements of Operations
(in thousands, except per share amounts)

| | THREE MONTHS ENDED DECEMBER 31, | |
	2000	1999
Revenues	$18,665	$16,712
Cost of revenues	6,789	4,935
Gross margin	11,876	11,777
Operating expenses:		
Product development and technology	1,956	1,331
Sales and marketing	10,810	17,635
Sales and marketing—NBC expenses	640	5,288
General and administrative	4,674	3,878
Depreciation and amortization	4,155	11,467
Impairment of goodwill	—	—
Total operating expenses	22,235	39,599
Loss from operations	(10,359)	(27,822)
Interest income, net	1,066	1,636
Other income, net	72	142
Writedown of investments	(317)	—
Loss from unconsolidated joint venture	(307)	—
Net loss from continuing operations	(9,845)	(26,044)
Preferred stock deemed dividend	—	—
Net loss attributable to common stock-holders from continuing operations	(9,845)	(26,044)
Discontinued operations	(195)	(3,888)
Net loss attributable to common stockholders	$(10,040)	$(29,932)
Basic and diluted net loss per share attributable to common shareholders from continuing operations, excluding impairment of goodwill and writedown of investments	$(0.32)	$(0.91)
Basic and diluted net loss per share attributable to common shareholders	$(0.34)	$(1.04)
Weighted average shares of common stock outstanding used in computing basic and diluted net loss per share	29,707	28,660

iVILLAGE, INC., AND SUBSIDIARIES
Condensed Consolidated Balance Sheets
(in thousands)

	DECEMBER 31, 2000	DECEMBER 31, 1999
ASSETS		
Current assets:		
Cash and cash equivalents	$48,963	$106,010
Restricted cash	—	1,495
Accounts receivable, net	7,864	6,620
Inventory	—	2,332
Other current assets	9,700	3,193
Total current assets	66,527	119,650
Restricted cash	9,250	—
Fixed assets, net	20,057	10,017
Goodwill and intangible assets, net	36,432	175,143
Other assets	137	7,938
Non-current assets of discontinued operations	56	—
Total assets	$132,459	$312,748
LIABILITIES:		
Current liabilities:		
Accounts payable and accrued expenses	$18,695	$16,216
Deferred revenue	6,337	12,682
Deferred rent	361	—
Net current liabilities of discontinued operations	882	—
Total current liabilities	26,275	28,898
Deferred rent, net of current portion	4,818	—
Total liabilities	31,093	28,898

Now look at expenses: they exceed revenues by nearly 20 percent—an improvement over the prior year, to be sure, but still a long way from where they need to be given iVillage's revenues. In fact, though the company cut its sales and marketing expenses drastically (by more than 50 percent), that single line item still equals more than 60 percent of what iVillage took in as revenues. iVillage's cash balance is an even bigger problem—at less than $49 million, it has fallen by more than half over the past year. Assuming no let-up in its burn rate, the company has barely four quarters to get profitable, raise more money, or go out of business. Indeed, in the press release accompanying its financial report, iVillage promises to turn cash-flow positive within three quarters. But iVillage also warns of expected "overall softness" in the advertising market in 2001—a theme common to advertising-dependent Internet companies, but which appears to have affected iVillage far more than it affected Yahoo! during the prior three months.

A closer read of the press release accompanying iVillage's financial report will give you some indication of its popularity and stickiness, important factors for the success of any community-oriented Web site. The company boasts, for example, that it ranks well in terms of both page views and "length of stay" at the site. But while you can read this sort of thing if you find it interesting, it's not mandatory. What you need to know, you can find out from the top and bottom lines. Leave it to the advertisers to figure out whether iVillage's Web site is popular enough or sticky enough to warrant their advertising dollars. All you need to worry about is whether the company is selling ads.

All in all, iVillage earns a C minus for the quarter. Sales are up, but only marginally, and the overall number is still tiny. More important, the company's cash position, while not dire, isn't all that great either. The only investor to whom this stock should be appealing is one who loves the site and truly believes in the product—or who has a near-suicidal urge to take risks. At this point, its financial statements suggest that iVillage probably never will be a company with big revenues and profits—at least not anytime in the foreseeable future.

So How Do I Pick?

You're almost there. The good news is that you now know a good bit about how consumer-oriented Internet companies work, what they're trying to accomplish, and how to understand their financial reports. The bad news is that that was the easy part. The hard part is picking which ones to invest in. It's hard because it's not just about numbers and which company earns the most—that's easy to figure out. Instead, it's about taking that information and combining it with a host of other factors, including your own investment needs and objectives. Here are three steps you should take before putting your dollars to work. Following them won't guarantee that you'll pick a winner every time, but it should help you avoid a lot of losers. (And one more bit of good news: these guidelines are good for all sorts of companies, not just those in the B2C sector!)

First, figure out your objectives. Are you investing on a thirty-year horizon, or a five-year horizon? How much risk do you want to add to your overall portfolio? Keep in mind that no one stock should make up a disproportionate share of your investments, and that different investors should have different objectives, and hence portfolios with different risk-return ratios. If your time horizon is shorter and your tolerance for risk less, you probably shouldn't be investing in a company such as buy.com, with an unproven business model and a long road to profitability. On the other hand, if you can afford to wait a few years, and take on some more risk, you may not need the safety net of a Wal-Mart or Kmart, which have a track record of profitability, but also a likelihood of slower growth in the future.

Second, use common sense. The Internet is a great thing, but don't let yourself be seduced by it. For starters, don't invest in a business you would otherwise never consider just because it's suddenly on-line. Take pet supplies as an example. It isn't exactly a growth industry. In the United States, sales of pet supplies are rising at just 6 percent per year on average, according to the Pet Industry Joint Advisory Council. Much of that business may migrate on-line, and individual companies may have faster growth rates than others. The Internet may also make pet supply companies more efficient and more profitable. But don't kid yourself: a company that sells doggie sweaters isn't likely to be a barn burner, whether or not it does business on the Internet.

Third, do your homework. If you're going to pick your own stocks, you have to be prepared to do some work. Read the newspaper every day, watch the business news, and find out what the experts think about whatever company it is you're thinking of investing in. But don't stop there. Go on-line, and read the company's securities filings and quarterly reports yourself (you know what to look for now!). Most of this information should be available right on the company's own Web site. Here are some questions you should ask:

1. How strong is this company's management team? In general, companies run by their founders don't do well long-term. These people may have vision, but they often don't have day-to-day operational skills. Sometimes the clues are obvious, as with Value America's founder and former chairman, Craig Winn, who was ultimately ousted by that company's management as its sales failed to materialize and its stock sank. As Value America's initial public offering prospectus indicated, Winn had previously started a lighting fixture manufacturer and distributor that had gone bankrupt. (He also sold millions of dollars' worth of stock in the IPO, generally not a good sign.) Other times, the evidence is more subtle. Take Beyond.com founder and former CEO, Mark Breier—who also lost his job after the company failed to live up to expectations and its stock crashed. Breier's idea of selling software over the Net was a good one. And he was a gutsy marketer, once showing up in nothing more than boxer shorts for a national TV interview to garner publicity for his company. But he had little managerial experience, having previously never risen beyond vice president of marketing at Amazon, and he was unable to execute on his vision.

Of course, there are very few seasoned Internet company executives, because there are very few seasoned Internet companies. And it's probably not wise to ignore "the vision thing" entirely. So look for companies whose founders are still around, but whose top executives have had experience in similar positions at other successful firms. Consider Amazon.com. Its founder, chairman, and CEO, Jeff Bezos, never ran a retailer before thinking up Amazon. But he did have considerable experience on Wall Street, and many of his top executives did have extensive real-world experience before joining Amazon, including Chief Financial Officer Warren Jenson, who previously held the same position at NBC and Delta Airlines. Another example: eBay founder Pierre Omidyar, who lacked significant management expertise before coming up with eBay as a nifty way to trade Pez dispensers on the Web. But CEO Meg Whitman previously ran Hasbro's preschool division and served as president of FTD, while Chief Technology Officer Maynard Webb held a similar post at Gateway. A third example: priceline.com founder Jay Walker, a creative inventor but not a veteran of managing big companies. Priceline.com Chairman Richard Braddock, though, was a former president of Citicorp, and CEO Dan Schulman was a senior executive at AT&T. Amazon, eBay, and priceline.com are all considered well-managed Internet retailers. (This doesn't necessarily mean they are safe investments. Skeptics have raised questions about the sustainability of all three business models—and Priceline in particular has had execution problems. Still, an experienced management team is a good indicator of likely future success—if not exactly a guarantee.)

Company Snapshot: priceline.com

At a Glance
Ticker symbol: PCLN
Founded: 1998
Went public: 1999
2000 revenue: $1.24 billion
Revenue growth rate (vs. 1999): 156.1%
2000 losses: $36.1 million
Profit growth rate (vs. 1999): NA
Key management: Richard Braddock, Chairman;
Dan Schulman, President and Chief Executive Officer

Founded by entrepreneur Jay Walker, priceline.com is a business built on a great idea and a questionable patent. The idea: to allow customers to "name their own price" for goods and services, and to match those bids against an inventory of goods and services provided by a variety of vendors, in search of a potential match. Customers who are highly sensitive to price, but less concerned about brand or other factors, can be paired with vendors seeking to unload an excess inventory of perishable products, without slashing prices across the board.

Here's how it works: Say you're looking for a cheap airfare between New York and Los Angeles. You bid $150, committing to spend that much for a ticket that gets you between those two locations on dates you specify. Airline X, whose published fares are $300 for that route, tells Priceline it will accept bids as low as, say, $140. Your bid gets matched with Airline X—but you get placed on a flight of the airline's choice and may have to make a stop or two on the way. The airline thus unloads a ticket that would otherwise go unused without lowering its published fares, while you, the customer, can buy a ticket cheaper than you would otherwise but lose out on the choice of an airline, the route, and the exact travel times.

Priceline, which makes money by charging a commission on each sale, has proved popular with consumers. That has prompted competitors, ranging from the Expedia travel service to some of the very same airlines that participate in the Priceline service, to set up competing sites. And that raises the question of whether Priceline, which has a patent on its "name your own price" method, is a self-sustaining business in its own right or simply a *means* of doing business, like an auction or a sale.

So far, the evidence is decidedly mixed. Priceline's effort to sell excess airline tickets has been successful—though how big a business that might ultimately become and how dependent it is on airline cooperation remain open to question. Fans argue that, given time, the Priceline model can be used to sell just about anything. But efforts to apply the model beyond airline tickets—to gasoline, groceries, and used goods—have failed. That leads skeptics to argue that Priceline is little more than a discount travel agency. And even that business, they contend, will prove difficult in the face of serious competition from the airlines themselves.

2. What's the company's track record? Find out from press reports how well the company has lived up to its own performance
targets—and Wall Street's expectations—in the recent past. Does it
have a track record of meeting or beating quarterly earnings estimates? What about its revenue growth? Remember: no retailer can
make money without selling products for more than they cost.
Check out the company's gross profit margin. It's probably the
most important figure to look at in a retailer's income statement
after revenues and profits. Is it negative (meaning the company
loses money on every sale)? Or is it positive? If so, how big a number is it, and is it shrinking or growing? Keep in mind that many
profitable retailers have gross margins north of 30 percent, and a
handful have margins north of 50 percent.

3. How big a market does the company hope to address? What
are the competitive characteristics of that market?

Read any initial public offering prospectus, and it'll include
hyperbolic language about the size of any company's market opportunity. Take these estimates with a heaping spoonful of salt—
and don't forget competition. The U.S. pet supplies market may be
worth close to $30 billion a year—but what is any one pet supply
retailer's share of that market? And what does that share suggest
about the maximum amount that company can ever be worth?

4. Who are the investors in this company, and what is their
track record? How much cash does the firm have on hand? How
long can the site hold out if the capital markets collapse and its ability to raise new funds is diminished or delayed?

It takes money to make money, and that's as true on the Internet as it is anywhere else. Because of the unbridled enthusiasm investors have at times displayed for Internet stocks, companies have
gone public at far earlier stages in their life cycle than ever before.
That means investors in those companies have assumed a far
greater risk than before that they won't live up to expectations and
thousands of investors have, in fact, been burned. One way of min-
imizing that risk is by evaluating who the original, pre-IPO investors are and how well their other investments have performed.
(Past performance, as they say, is no guarantee of future performance—but it's often a good indicator.) Another important factor
is a company's time horizon to expected profitability and self-

sufficiency—its "path to profitability," in Internet-speak. Check out the firm's quarterly earnings report to see how much money the company has on hand, how quickly it's burning through that money, and what kind of ability it has to conserve cash if it needs to. (Remember: fixed overhead costs, such as salaries, leases, and debt payments, are a lot harder to trim in a hurry than variable overhead costs, such as advertising and marketing.)

Once you've gone through all these steps, then and only then should you start thinking about what's an appropriate price to buy the stock. Using valuation steps we'll outline in greater detail in Chapter Seven, you'll take your estimates of the company's future market share, revenues, profitability, and price-to-earnings ratio, and calculate what an appropriate value might be for the stock over the time horizon you have in mind. Then you'll discount that price back using your required rate of return and *voilà!* you'll have figured out the price you're willing to pay to own the stock.

Company Snapshot: E*TRADE

At a Glance
Ticker symbol: ET
Founded: 1992
Went public: 1996
Fiscal 2000 revenue: $739.1 million (year ended Sept. 30)
Revenue growth rate (vs. 1999): 108%
Fiscal 2000 losses: $19.1 million (year ended Sept. 30)
Profit growth rate (vs. 1999): NA
Key management: Christos Cotsakos, Chairman and CEO

One of the biggest of the on-line brokerage firms—along with Charles Schwab and Ameritrade—E*TRADE has been closely identified with the dot-com euphoria. It is, after all, an Internet company itself—but it is an Internet company that allows customers to trade in the stocks of other companies. And what kinds of companies do E*TRADE investors most like to invest in? That's right, Internet companies. Perhaps not surprisingly, one of the most heavily traded stocks among E*TRADE customers in the past has been that of E*TRADE itself.

As a brokerage firm, E*TRADE benefits from heavy trading volumes. The more its customers trade, the more it earns in brokerage fees—even if those fees are a small fraction of what they are at full-service brokerage firms. The risk, of course, is that if the markets head south and trading volumes sag, E*TRADE's fortunes are likely to sag with them. In response to that risk, E*TRADE and other on-line brokerages have sought to diversify their revenue streams beyond trading. In E*TRADE's case, that has meant selling mutual funds and buying both an on-line bank (Telebanc, subsequently renamed E*TRADE Bank) and a national network of automated teller machines. The catch is that in the short term, on-line banking has proved far less popular with consumers than on-line trading. Over the long term, however, E*TRADE hopes to profit by capturing a larger and larger "wallet share" from its customers, thereby earning money from them no matter how they choose to invest their own.

One final word of caution: after you've made your purchase, forget about it for a while. Give yourself a break and your company time to perform. Sure, you might want to check up on your stock every once in a while, just to make sure it hasn't fallen off a cliff—or gone through the roof. But if you worry about every gyration, you'll drive yourself nuts. That goes not just for consumer-oriented dot coms, like the ones we studied in this chapter, but for all Net stocks—and really for all non-Net stocks as well. Remember: investing for your own account is partly about making the most of your money and partly about having fun. If you're not having fun, and if you're not prepared to make mistakes once in a while, then you shouldn't be a stock picker.

Moving On

So much for the consumer Net stocks. In one sense, they're the most fun to learn about and invest in, because they're the companies we're most familiar with in our daily lives. After all, if you're considering buying shares of Amazon.com, you've probably shopped there. And if you haven't, you probably have no business owning the stock!

But as familiar as they are—and as much attention as they receive in the mass media—consumer companies account for only a small fraction of the business that's conducted on the Web, and they make up only a tiny part of the Internet universe. In the next few chapters, we'll explore a host of companies and business models that are probably a lot less familiar to you and that may, for that reason, be more challenging to get your arms around. But as you'll see, that shouldn't, in and of itself, make them any less appealing as potential investments.

CHAPTER FOUR

Now You're Talking Money

*The Business of
Business to Business*

You've heard the old saying "A million here, a million there, and pretty soon you're talking about real money." Substitute the word "billion" for "million," and you're talking about the business of business-to-business: selling goods and services to *corporate* customers—or setting up businesses that let them exchange goods and services with one another. Nicknamed "B2B" e-commerce, it's the least glamorous part of the virtual economy. It's also by far the biggest and arguably the most revolutionary.

What's included in B2B e-commerce? Basically, it's any form of on-line trade—of goods or of services—where both the buyer and the seller are companies rather than individuals. That includes all sorts of service companies, most operating behind the scenes, without which many other companies wouldn't be able to function on the Web: consulting firms that help off-line companies figure out on-line strategies and help on-line companies figure out how to serve their customers better; advertising companies that distribute advertisements across networks of Web sites; and "trade exchanges"—new, totally virtual gathering places where corporate buyers and sellers can come together, in cyberspace, to do business. By some definitions, it also includes the infrastructure companies that build the Internet's physical backbone, since, technically speaking, they are companies whose clients are other companies. For our purposes, though, I've broken those infrastructure companies out into a separate chapter, since the business models and investment qualities of those companies are very different from the more "virtual" B2B models I'll deal with in this chapter.

How big a business is B2B, both off-line and on-line? According to some estimates, companies will one day sell *ten times* the amount of goods and services to one another on-line as they will sell to individual consumers. Exactly what that translates into in hard numbers is a bit fuzzy, because it depends on a wide range of assumptions. But according to the experts at Goldman Sachs—who are paid a pretty penny to come up with these kinds of educated guesses—sales by U.S. companies in 1997 totaled $19.3 trillion, while the gross domestic product totaled just $8.3 trillion (including both on-line and off-line sales). The $11 trillion difference, Goldman concludes, was for "transfers" of goods and services—in other words, business-to-business sales of one sort or another. Goldman believes that number will increase to $13.7 trillion by 2004. And Goldman estimates that the U.S. gross domestic product accounts for less than a quarter of *global* GDP. That suggests more than $50 *trillion* in total B2B commerce around the world by the year 2003.

Most of that is still off-line. As of the year 2000, Goldman calculates that less than 0.5 percent of goods and services transfers happened electronically, a percentage that will almost certainly grow by leaps and bounds, even as the overall pie gets bigger. In the United States alone, Goldman estimates that B2B e-commerce totaled $115 billion in 1999, a figure it predicts will surge to $1.1 trillion in 2003. A competing estimate, by International Data Corporation, puts 1999 U.S. B2B e-commerce at $50 billion—and $80 billion globally—numbers it forecasts will rise to $633 billion and $1.1 trillion, respectively, by 2003. A third firm, Forrester Research, estimates that B2B e-commerce in the United States totaled $109 billion in 1999 and will jump to $1.3 trillion by 2003. And some people think all those estimates are too conservative. In any event, it isn't the specific numbers that should interest us, it's the awe-some potential for growth.

Beyond the sheer volume of business that will soon be trans-acted on-line is the incredible ripple effect that transferring that business from the off-line world will have on the economy. If sell-ing books and refrigerators to individuals on-line eliminates all sorts of middlemen whose job it was to sell books and refrigerators in the "real" world, how many jobs will be eliminated when *com-panies* cut way back on buyers and salespeople? And if on-line comparison shopping means lower retail prices for those books and refrigerators, imagine what those lower prices might mean when magnified to the billions of dollars giant corporations spend buying parts and supplies. Researchers at Morgan Stanley call the explo-sion of e-commerce "the second industrial revolution"—a revo-lution that, as they put it, is "about much greater efficiency in markets and in the flow of commerce."

An Unlikely Trio: A Case Study

Let's look at one example for an idea of what this can mean in prac-tical terms. In February 2000, the world's three largest carmakers— General Motors, Ford, and DaimlerChrysler—announced that they would create a single on-line marketplace for all their parts pur-chases. That announcement, as much as any other single event, demonstrated the immense impact the Internet is having on the business world. Sitting next to one another on a Detroit stage, cam-eras rolling and lightbulbs flashing, executives from the three com-panies acknowledged that the Internet had, in just a few months, forced them to realize what decades of bitter competition hadn't: that by working together in certain areas, they could improve the efficiency and profitability of the entire carmaking industry.

Barely four months earlier, Ford and GM had each announced plans to create their own, rival on-line purchasing exchanges— Ford together with Oracle, GM with a start-up called Commerce One. DaimlerChrysler was also looking for a technology partner to launch an on-line parts-buying program. But an outcry from their suppliers—many of whom sold goods and services to all the automakers—caused the companies to realize that forcing their partners to do business on several exchanges would be very inefficient and might discourage some suppliers from participating. By combining their efforts, the car companies could guarantee that their suppliers would join the network, making the exchange much more useful. And by establishing the marketplace as a separate unit outside their companies—while each owning a piece of it—the companies hoped to make big bucks in the stock market. They announced plans to spin the business out in an initial public stock offering before they had even figured out a name (ultimately, Covisint was their choice). And within hours, they had received phone calls from rivals in Europe and Japan asking about getting in on the venture.

Even in Internet terms, the scale of the undertaking is huge. General Motors alone said it intended to use the Web exchange to order roughly $50 billion worth of parts during the venture's first year—*more than three times the total annual amount of consumer commerce on the Internet at the time.* Together with their suppliers, the three companies estimated that the platform could easily manage *more than half a trillion dollars' worth* of buying and selling within a few years! Now, how exciting does the pet supplies business seem in comparison?

Of course, the new venture wouldn't just be about buying and selling. It would also revolutionize how the car-manufacturing business works. It would allow car companies to maintain closer contact with their suppliers and dealers. It would allow suppliers to receive and execute orders faster—without costly and time-consuming face-to-face meetings—while allowing carmakers to stockpile lower inventories. Ultimately, it would allow more cars to be bought and built on a made-to-order basis, with each customer's preferences instantly relayed to the manufacturer and its suppliers—avoiding the process of searching for off-the-shelf cars that match the buyer's tastes. And the whole process would be global, complete with automatic language and currency translation features, allowing participants to use it anywhere in the world.

Still, purchasing efficiency would be at the heart of the plan. By placing all their orders on a single Web marketplace, rival manufacturers could potentially attract more suppliers—and better prices—for each product than they would have simply by picking up the phone and calling around. Suppliers could pool their orders for products, extracting bulk discounts from their own vendors. And the exchange would allow buyers and sellers to conduct auctions and reverse auctions, potentially reducing costs even further. Though skeptics argue that the expectations for the venture are too great—after all, they say, it isn't as though Ford, GM, and Daimler-Chrysler haven't wrung steep price concessions out of their suppliers already—fans gush that it could single-handedly help control inflation by holding down the cost of new-car purchases.

Now imagine that process multiplied across such industries as aerospace, paper products, chemicals, and steel. In each case, by making information electronically available to all members of a supply chain, by offering new, more open procedures for bidding on contracts, and by reducing the need for face-to-face contact, the Internet offers the ability to cut waste and improve competition. Product development times can be shortened, customization increased, just-in-time manufacturing refined, inventories reduced, and costs lowered. It isn't hard to see where enthusiasts get the idea that, in the B2B space alone, the Net could reshape the global economy in ways as fundamental as electricity or even the wheel.

Company Snapshot: i2 Technologies

At a Glance
Ticker symbol: ITWO
Founded: 1988
Went public: 1996
2000 revenue: $1.1 billion
Revenue growth rate (vs. 1999): 97%
2000 profits: $108.4 million
Profit growth rate (vs. 1999): 252%
Key management: Sanjiv Sidhu, Chairman and CEO

i2 Technologies was originally created to develop software that helps companies manage their inventories. It evolved, with the advent of the commercial Internet, into a provider of technology that not only helps companies track inventories, but manage and procure products along their entire supply chains—all the raw materials they need to manufacture finished goods. Among other things, this technology helps improve the precision of just-in-time manufacturing systems, allowing customers to operate at peak efficiency.

Though it boasts many giant customers, i2's biggest clients include United Technologies and Honeywell (now part of General Electric), which retained i2 to help develop their MyAircraft on-line marketplace for the aerospace industry, where tens of billions of dollars' worth of parts and supplies are bought and sold.

The company's growth has been explosive. Between 1995 and 2000, i2's revenues rose more than twenty-fold, and they continue to rise at a rapid clip.

If It Were That Easy . . .

Before we get down to the nuts and bolts of what various B2B companies do and how they work, let's take a look at some of the major differences between B2B commerce and B2C commerce. In the last chapter, we discovered that pretty much anybody can set up a Web site claiming to sell something and call themselves an on-line retailer. Successful e-tailers are those that can build a brand, attract customers to their site, and get those customers to keep coming back and spending money.

In the B2B world, the requirements for success are very different. For one thing, brand name is a lot less important, which is why you don't see a lot of B2B companies advertising on TV and on highway billboards. On the other hand, customer service is much more important. As Morgan Stanley analysts put it, "An Amazon-like message that something 'usually ships in two to three days' won't cut it in B2B," when the part being ordered might play a vital role in some manufacturing process. Fulfillment—the process of getting an item from the supplier to the customer in good shape and on a tight schedule—is critical.

There are other differences as well. Unlike the relationship be-

tween an e-tailer and an individual consumer, relationships between companies generally are long-term, spelled out in detailed
contracts, and involve many layers of approvals on both sides before they're formalized. The reason for all that complexity is that
the size of the purchases is often huge, running to many millions of
dollars. Prices aren't set in stone, they're negotiated. Payments
aren't made just by credit card; often they involve wire transfers or
complex lines of credit. All that makes the average B2B transaction
a lot different from the impulse purchase of a book for $9.95 on
barnesandnoble.com.

What does that mean from an investor standpoint? In very
general terms, it means that B2B companies tend to spend a lot less
on advertising and marketing, but a lot more on sales and customer
service. That can add up to greater efficiency—but it can also mean
less flexibility about spending patterns (it's easier, after all, to pare
back an ad budget than it is to lay off a sales staff). It means that relationships with individual clients can be critical, with a single account contributing a meaningful percentage of revenues. That can
produce a higher risk of a sudden revenue shortfall when an account expires. On the other hand, having signed contracts in hand
means that revenues can often, with a fair degree of certainty, be
predicted for some time into the future. That can add up to better
predictability of performance—what Wall Street analysts like to
call "visibility."

Company Snapshot: WebMD

At a Glance
Ticker symbol: HLTH
Founded: 1996
Went public: 1999
2000 revenue: $318.2 million (through fiscal Q3)
Revenue growth rate (vs. 1999): 362%
2000 losses: $194.3 million (through fiscal Q3)
Profit growth rate (vs. 1999): NA
Key management: Martin Wygod, CEO

Formed from the merger of three large companies—Healtheon, WebMD, and Medical Manager—as well as a host of smaller ones, the company now known as WebMD started out with the grand vision that it would one day link doctors, patients, insurers, and other medical professionals in a giant, highly efficient on-line network. Each of the companies brought a different expertise to the equation. Healtheon, founded by Jim Clark, the founder of both Netscape and Silicon Graphics, aimed to unite doctors, hospitals, and insurers, allowing them to exchange patient files and insurance authorizations on-line. WebMD, led by a youthful Internet entrepreneur named Jeffrey Arnold, focused its Web site at individual consumers, hoping to empower them with vast amounts of previously hard to obtain medical information. And Medical Manager, headed by a savvy businessman named Martin Wygod, had its origins as a software company, whose products were used by large numbers of physicians to manage their medical practices. The goal of bringing all three together was to increase the availability of medical information and decrease the massive amounts of bureaucracy and paperwork involved in health care.

Though that vision remains in place, the early results have not been entirely encouraging. Physicians, it turns out, have been slower to embrace the Internet and move their practice information on-line than was originally hoped. Insurers have been similarly slow, as well as reluctant to pay a third party to help them process claims and information. And while consumers are heading on-line in droves to obtain medical information, it's not entirely clear how to make money from their interest other than advertising. Nevertheless WebMD is still trying—aiming now to gradually move physicians who use its practice management software on-line while seeking to make money on the consumer end in part by selling medical news and information to Web sites and other companies for a fee. Messrs. Arnold and Clark have left the company, which is now run by Mr. Wygod alone.

Mikey Likes It: The B2B Conundrum

Within the business-to-business space, there is a huge variety of different business models. But most B2B companies present investors with similar challenges. For those inclined to the Warren Buffett school of money management—put your money to work in companies you know, whose products you use and like, and whose businesses you understand—B2B investments should be off limits. After all, most of us will never have any reason to use the VerticalNet on-line chemicals marketplace, and it's tough for us to really grasp what the "product" is that a consulting firm such as Viant, or even an advertising network such as DoubleClick, sells. While consumer companies are easy to understand because they aim their products squarely at us—and because most of us have an opinion as to whether those products are something we like or would ever buy—B2B companies are more obscure (notwithstanding everything you're reading in this chapter!).

But here's the flip side of that argument: there are certain qualities that most B2B e-commerce companies share that make them extremely attractive investments. First, because so many of them are really service companies, they don't have the overhead costs involved with selling physical products. Unlike Amazon.com, which buys goods at a wholesale price, stores them in a warehouse, and then sells them at a markup, the main "product" of most B2B e-commerce firms is plain old brainpower. By and large, that makes for lower revenues but higher profit margins. Amazon.com, for example, is by most accounts unlikely to have long-term operating profit margins higher than 8 or 9 percent; Viant, by contrast, is estimated to have long-term margins in the range of 15 percent and higher. Not selling a physical product also means these businesses are highly "scalable"—Internet-speak for "easy to grow." If a particular item proves popular, Amazon.com can sell more of it only if it can find and buy more of it and find a place to store it until it sells. That requires more warehouse space and a bigger distribution infrastructure. But to sell more consulting services, a consulting firm such as Viant only has to work its staff harder and find more smart people willing to work for it. In theory, at least, there's no limit to how big it can get, and taking on more business doesn't require a lot in the way of additional investment.

Another reason many B2B companies make good investments is that they're inherently viral. This is particularly true of a trade exchange, such as the one set up by the Big Three. The bigger an exchange gets, the more useful it becomes for both buyers and sellers. The more useful it becomes, the more buyers and sellers are likely to use it—making it, once again, that much more useful. Finally, for many B2B companies, the barriers to entry are relatively high. Unlike the consumer e-tail business—where anybody can set up a Web site selling just about any kind of product—many areas of the B2B sector are tough to break into. DoubleClick, for example, is a powerful advertising network because of the huge number of client sites that use it to fill their available space with ads; those clients are bound to DoubleClick contractually, making it much harder for any start-up to take on DoubleClick as a competitor. In the same way, the Big Three auto parts exchange, which is operated at a nuts-and-bolts technology level by Oracle and Commerce One, has locked up the world's largest car companies as its clients. Any would-be rivals are essentially frozen out of the business before they even get started. (This isn't true of the consulting side of the B2B business; just about anybody, after all, can set up shop as a "consultant," and consulting contracts are generally not exclusive, though clients do tend to stick with consultants they know and like.)

Still, all this doesn't answer the tricky question: How do you judge a B2B company's prospects if you're totally unfamiliar with its products? Sure, you can tell that certain companies—such as Commerce One and DoubleClick—have a big market share. You can also look at a company's income statement and tell if it's making money, if its profit margins are strong, and if its revenues are growing. But how do you even know where to start? How do you know which companies to even look at? Here's the bad news: there's no easy way. Silly as it sounds, the best answer is to stay alert and keep your eyes and ears peeled. If you work for a company that does business on a Web-based trade exchange, find out which one and whether it's working well (if you work at one of the Big Three automakers, for example, you could gauge internal satisfaction with the products and services provided by Oracle and Commerce One). If your company advertises on the Internet, find out which advertising network it uses. If your company has used consultants to help improve its on-line operations, find out which consultants it has used and whether or not they were highly regarded. Ask your friends and colleagues. What consulting firm does their business use? What Web exchanges have they done business on? And, of course, read the paper and watch the business news to find out which B2B companies are emerging as major players. All this is far from a perfect solution. But remember, your objective isn't to come up with a comprehensive list of every company in the B2B space. You're simply trying to come up with a handful of long-term winners.

Trading Places: B2B Exchanges

We've already discussed one of the biggest of the so-called B2B trade exchanges—the car parts marketplace being established by the Big Three. But there are literally hundreds of other B2B trade exchanges in the works. By year-end 2002, according to one estimate, there will be five thousand in hundreds of different industries, many competing for the same business. Few of these will ever make it public, and most won't survive. Many will merge; others will simply fail. Researchers at Morgan Stanley note that, during its early years, the New York Stock Exchange had two dozen rivals in lower Manhattan alone. By the late twentieth century, it had one. Morgan Stanley calls this "the classic technology hype cycle." The cycle, as they describe it, has three phases: a "frenzy and land grab," followed by a long, slow maturation of the technology ("the hard part," during which the stock market euphoria cools off), followed by "the production phase," when the real benefits of the technology kick in, a few clear winners emerge, and the market gets excited again. Morgan Stanley warns that notwithstanding the huge promise all the trade exchanges offer, "the structural shift in the economy . . . will take years to play out." The bottom line:

Hold your horses. This thing will be huge, but it won't be huge overnight.

Company Snapshot: VerticalNet

At a Glance
Ticker symbol: VERT
Founded: 1995
Went public: 1999
2000 revenue: $154.7 million (through Q3)
Revenue growth rate (vs. 1999): 1351%
2000 losses: $48.7 million (through Q3)
Profit growth rate (vs. 1999): NA
Key management: Michael Hagan, President and Chief Executive Officer

Designed as a virtual meeting place where businesses across multiple industries can come together to buy and sell goods and services, VerticalNet operates its so-called vertical communities in a wide variety of different sectors from health care to food service to textiles to electronic components. The company has three areas of focus. It offers content—from news to classified ads and job listings to product information—within each of the various sectors. It offers "storefronts"—which it can help set up, for a fee, and for which it charges "rent"—where companies can offer their own products for sale. And it operates a series of trade exchanges, where companies can auction off various goods and services, and for which VerticalNet charges commissions.

VerticalNet has grown rapidly via acquisition, and indeed much of the company's revenues so far have derived from these acquired companies, many of whom do a significant chunk of their business off-line. Critics say the company can't hope to compete across such a broad spectrum of industries, against giant consortia set up by leading players in each of those industries. But believers in the Vertical-Net strategy argue that by focusing not on the giants within these industries but on the smaller players with annual revenues of $50 million or less, the company can carve out a profitable niche for itself.

VerticalNet has seen its own revenues grow rapidly, from less than $2 million in the first quarter of 1999 to an expected $100 million by the final quarter of 2001.

Before we get down to hard numbers, let's take a closer look at a hypothetical trade exchange transaction, to understand how these marketplaces can work at a nitty-gritty level. Let's say Acme Manufacturing needs three hundred tons of a certain type of steel. Before the advent of the Web, a purchasing representative from Acme Manufacturing would call around to various steel suppliers, specify the kind and quantity of steel he was looking for, and negotiate a price. Most likely, the purchasing representative would select from a list of companies with whom he'd previously done business, or that had been referred by a trusted source; perhaps he'd prioritize his calls according to which company he had the best relationship with—or which steel salesman he'd played golf with most recently. And then he'd haggle. With the Web, though, the purchasing representative doesn't have to find a list or pick up the phone. Instead, he can log on to an on-line exchange such as e-STEEL and simply comparison shop right there, finding the best offering from a selection of available suppliers. Alternatively, he can use a service like one offered by FreeMarkets to conduct a modified form of "reverse" auction, in which the steel suppliers themselves actually bid on his business. How's that for convenient? The Acme representative can post a request for three hundred tons of a certain type of steel on the marketplace and simply wait for the bids to show up. At the end of the bidding, the best price will have presented itself. This style of doing business isn't just easier, with improved selection and, in theory at least, better, more transparent pricing than the old method; it also is faster, permits more informed decision making, and is fundamentally more fair. Companies that might never have known Acme's business was available, or that may not have had a historic relationship with it, can now compete for its business. What's more, the back-slapping, martini-drinking, one-hand-washes-the-other personal relationship is totally eliminated. Steel manufacturers that may never have showed up on Acme's radar screen—or may have struggled to establish the personal contacts that help grease the wheels of business in the physical world—can compete on a completely even playing field in the virtual world. In cyberspace, their bid can't be distinguished from their rivals' bids on anything other than merit.

How much can this process yield in the way of savings? According to British Telecom, shifting its procurement on-line has cut costs from $113 to an astounding $8 per transaction. More broadly, according to Morgan Stanley, the cost of processing a typical purchase order manually ranges from $125 to $175, an amount that can be reduced by $10 to $15 by moving the process on-line. Of course, that doesn't account for the actual savings in product costs. That will vary from industry to industry and from product to product. In some cases, it will undoubtedly be considerable. Then again, let's keep things in perspective: most giant corporations have been buying and selling the same sorts of products, from the same group of suppliers, for years. They've negotiated and haggled and argued over prices for a very long time. In some cases, they may be willing—knowingly—to pay more in exchange for something unique, or something with a particular brand name. Moving the process on-line may therefore save on process costs and time, but it won't necessarily make *every* product cheaper right away. As the authors of Morgan Stanley's *B2B Internet Report* put it, on-line B2B exchanges probably won't yield the kind of massive price deflation that would cause the world economy to "implode." But the greater transparency such exchanges allow *should* create more uniform pricing and fewer price discrepancies.

Some giant companies—like the Big Three—have set up their own purchasing exchanges, using firms such as Oracle, Commerce One, i2 Technologies, Ariba, or FreeMarkets to create and operate these on-line marketplaces for them. In other cases, the marketplaces have been developed independently of the firms that use them. VerticalNet, for example, offers exchanges for a variety of different products from industrial chemicals to plastics. VerticalNet itself doesn't buy or sell any of those products. Instead, just as the Nasdaq Stock Market offers an electronic forum for buying and selling stocks, the company simply provides a place where corporate buyers and sellers of products can meet on-line, exchange information, negotiate prices, and enter into contracts, all without face-to-face contact. VerticalNet itself makes money from participation fees, as well as transaction commissions.

Exactly how profitable these exchanges will become isn't clear. Originally, it appeared that the exchanges could charge membership fees, transaction fees, and commissions. But what the auto parts exchange made clear is that, as old-world companies start to throw their weight around—or even set up their own exchanges— that kind of pricing structure probably won't last. And even if it were to last, it's questionable how profitable a business could be if its main source of income derived from shaving a tiny sliver off of every transaction (even though the transactions add up). Consider: according to Morgan Stanley, the New York Stock Exchange handled well over $7 trillion in trading volume in 1998, yet its revenues totaled just $100 million that year. The lesson: the big money isn't made simply matching buy and sell orders. For trade exchanges doing business in a single industry, becoming very profitable requires developing other sources of income. For exchanges doing business in multiple industries—such as Commerce One, which is helping to set up exchanges not just in the auto industry but also in aerospace and financial services, among others—the situation is perhaps less dire, since transaction volume can add up to multiple trillions quite quickly. Even for those companies, though, long-term revenue and profit growth means unearthing other sources of income, including ongoing service and support fees for helping to manage the exchange's technological infrastructure.

Company Snapshot: Ariba

At a Glance
Ticker symbol: ARBA
Founded: 1996
Went public: 1999
Fiscal 2000 revenue: $279 million (year ended Sept. 30)
Revenue growth rate (vs. 1999): 515%
Fiscal 2000 losses: $29.5 million (year ended Sept. 30)
Profit growth rate (vs. 1999): NA
Key management: Keith Krach, Chairman and CEO

One of the leaders in the business-to-business sector, Ariba is a software company that provides the technology underlying many of the leading trade exchanges. Its customers range from Sabre, the travel reservations systems company, to Cargill, the grain processor. Key competitors include Commerce One, as well as, to some extent, Oracle and SAP.

Ariba's software automates much of the work that was previously handled by corporate procurement officers charged with buying and selling goods and services. The software is used by trade exchanges to list products available for sale, as well as to manage the buying and selling, often in the form of auctions. Within corporations, Ariba's software is also used for tracking orders and managing purchasing procedures.

Though it is often compared with VerticalNet and i2 Technologies, Ariba is actually not a direct competitor of either company. It doesn't provide the same type of content for vertical communities as does VerticalNet, nor does it focus on managing supply chains, as does i2—though some observers suggest it may have its eye on i2's turf.

Two Heads Are Better Than One

Despite the fact that major industrial giants are increasingly trying to use their clout to exercise control over the budding trade exchanges, their dependence on third parties to build and operate these electronic marketplaces is noteworthy. The lesson: though these giant companies know their industries backwards and forwards, and though their participation has the power to make or break the new trade exchanges, they lack the expertise to make the transition to the new economy on their own. They need help. And that lesson, as it turns out, has ramifications well beyond trade exchanges, to all sorts of far-flung corners of the business world.

To get some sense of how significant those ramifications are, consider all the non-Internet companies in the United States. Now think about how many of those firms need to develop Internet sites and Internet strategies. Finally, think of how few of those firms—

from the very smallest to the very largest—will be able to suddenly become Internet-savvy on their own. That'll give you some taste of how big the opportunity is for Internet consulting, the business of helping off-line firms create Web sites, develop on-line strategies, and implement new, Internet-related technologies, while helping on-line firms grow and run their businesses better. According to Goldman Sachs, in previous technology cycles, "organizations adopted new technology when it was convenient. Now, virtually every organization is being forced to formulate an e-business strategy immediately." Paranoid about being left behind, many are also unsure what to do about it. Enter the e-business consultants. Large corporations, in particular, are committing huge sums of money to dot-com consulting projects: tens, if not hundreds, of millions of dollars at a pop. That's created a market for Internet consultants that's big and growing fast, with revenues jumping anywhere from 50 percent to 75 percent annually, from about $20 billion in 2000 to an estimated $65 billion by 2003. While there are a few giants in the business, the consulting industry is actually highly fragmented. That, combined with such rapid market growth, means that more than a few consulting firms have a tremendous potential for growth.

A caveat: not all Internet consultants are actually Internet companies themselves. While a lot of consulting firms will profit from the transition to an Internet economy—hiring professionals who specialize in developing Internet strategies and even creating Internet consulting divisions—only a few firms are primarily focused on Internet consulting or were built in the Internet age. What's more, like many professional services firms—physicians' practices, law partnerships, and advertising agencies come to mind—many consulting firms are private companies or partnerships. These include some of the most prestigious names in the consulting business: Accenture (formerly Andersen Consulting), Bain & Company, the Boston Consulting Group (BCG), and McKinsey & Company. On the other hand, many among the new breed of dot-com consultants have decided to hop on the IPO bandwagon, milking the stock market for capital and becoming publicly traded companies in the process. Happily for investors, that spells o-p-p-o-r-t-u-n-i-t-y.

Not all consultants are identical, and while we don't need to get into a lot of detail about the nitty-gritty of the consulting business, it's worth a quick overview to understand some of the key differences. (A given consulting firm's Web site—or its financial filings—should identify which of the following categories it falls under.) First, some consultants are what is known as "vertically" focused, meaning they specialize in one area or have specialized project teams, while others are "horizontally" structured, meaning they adopt a more generalist approach. While some analysts think that vertically structured firms have a better shot at winning work based on their expertise, such specialization also increases risk by associating a firm with a particular kind of technology or project. Second, while most consultants bill out their services in the same way lawyers do—at an hourly rate plus expenses—some consultants are beginning to experiment with new pricing mechanisms, realizing that clients can be uncomfortable with the thought of an unlimited bill from a consultant whose financial incentive is to spend as much time and money as possible on a project. As a result, some firms have adopted fixed pricing structures, in which they bid on entire projects and charge a flat fee for the work. While this may end up costing the client more than paying by the hour, the benefit is that the fee is capped and there's no risk of an unexpected, enormous bill. Similarly, for the consultant there's an incentive to get the job done quickly, within an allotted time—though there is also some risk of a project proving trickier and more time-consuming than initially expected. Another billing method in the early stages of testing at some firms is called "value pricing," in which the consultant agrees to be compensated according to a percentage of revenues generated or expenses saved as a consequence of the consultant's work. Again, the idea here is to align the consultant's financial interests with those of the client. Some analysts favor these latter two approaches, because they believe that, if properly implemented, they can lead to fatter profits than the traditional method. That said, one big benefit of the consulting business is that it's flexible and opportunistic. If a firm realizes its vertical focus is limiting its opportunities, it can broaden that focus; if a client prefers to be billed a certain way, it's not a big problem to do so.

In fact, whichever pricing mechanism a consulting firm chooses, the consulting business itself is inherently profitable. It requires no big up-front investment in technology and no big infrastructure. All it does require is brainpower and the office space to house it. (Sometimes it doesn't even require that, as many consultants spend much of their time working from home or from their clients' offices. Goldman cites the example of one firm, Sapient, that opened an office in Europe only after it had attracted enough business there that the office would be guaranteed enough work to make it profitable.) Typically, well-run consulting firms have gross profit margins north of 50 percent, meaning that every additional dollar's worth of business costs less than 50 cents to supply, and operating profit margins in the high teens, meaning that after all expenses are deducted, 18 or 19 cents of every dollar in revenue drops to the bottom line. That isn't bad.

At least in an operational sense—if not always in the stock market—Internet consultants are arguably among the most reliable of dot-com investments because their success isn't dependent on any one business plan or any single technology. Instead, they help clients refine business plans of all types, choose which technologies to use, and integrate those technologies into their businesses. Consultants thus represent what are known as "proxy" investments—bets that the Internet will grow, thereby benefiting their business—without betting on the success or failure of any one business plan or technology (more on proxy investments in Chapter Six).

Consulting firms are also attractive businesses for two other reasons. First, competition isn't particularly intense. Not only is there a considerable demand for the kind of brainpower consultants can provide, but once a consultant wins an assignment, that assignment is likely to yield additional work with that same client with relatively little extra effort. According to Goldman, repeat customers account for more than half of Sapient's revenues, and the firm competes for just a quarter of its new business.

Second, the growth of any one consulting firm is, in theory at least, unlimited. Although it's true that a giant consulting firm is probably more unwieldy than a small boutique, there are a number of giant firms with tens of thousands of employees that operate quite successfully—and are getting bigger all the time. The trick is finding the firms that are well managed enough to pull that off. For investors, though, room to grow a business means room for an investment to grow in value.

Company Snapshot: Sapient

At a Glance
Ticker symbol: SAPE
Founded: 1991
Went public: 1996
2000 revenue: $503.3 million
Revenue growth rate (vs. 1999): 82%
2000 profits: $57.7 million
Profit growth rate (vs. 1999): 60%
Key management: Jerry Greenberg, J. Stuart Moore, Co-chairmen, Co-CEOs

One of the largest of the Internet consulting firms, Sapient was founded by two former consultants at Cambridge Technology Partners. Though its origins are in the more technical aspects of the business—particularly the development and integration of Internet systems with its clients' existing technology—Sapient has quickly expanded its offerings to include Web site design, branding, and content development. Thus, the company can now take a client's idea for an Internet company and build it from scratch, from the back-end systems to the front-end look and feel of the Web site—and, in fact, more than a few of its assignments consist of just that.

Though many of its rivals have run into trouble during venture capital and capital market droughts as their upstart clients have lost the funding necessary to keep their operations going, Sapient's client roster includes many blue-chip names. These established companies—from American Airlines to Caterpillar to General Motors—have turned to Sapient to build or improve their Internet operations and aren't likely to go out of business overnight, leaving their consulting bills unpaid.

What's more, Sapient has won the loyalty and good recommendations of many of its clients not just by earning a reputation for solid work, but also by keeping projects within their budgets. The company helped pioneer the fixed-time/fixed-price model for consulting projects, offering clients a choice of paying by the hour or paying a flat fee for an entire project. On occasion, that approach has cost Sapient money as projects have proved trickier and taken more time than originally expected. On the whole, though, it seems to have spurred Sapient's growth and its quick rise to profitability rather than hurt it.

In other ways, though, investors are taking on a huge risk when they put money in consulting firms, because, as trite as it sounds, the assets they're buying leave the office in the elevator every night. Consultants, after all, are people, and people take jobs and quit jobs in a not entirely predictable manner. So long as a consulting firm is doing well, it's likely to continue doing well, because it's likely to be a popular place to work. But all it may take is one stumble—a management change, say, or something that causes the stock price to slip—for discontent to worm its way in. And discontent has a way of festering that can also be disastrous; if it causes enough smart people to leave, a consulting firm's main assets can disappear overnight in a way that the physical assets of a retailer or a technology firm never could.

What does that mean for investors? It may mean nothing more than that—in the consulting business as in so many other businesses—the fastest growth also comes with the highest risk. Generally speaking, consulting firms are considered a relatively conservative way of betting indirectly on the growth of the Internet without putting all yours chips in one basket. The biggest potential for growth, naturally, is with the smaller firms that are in hyperexpansion mode—firms that are hot and winning new clients all the time, with each client adding measurably to the firm's success. These are also the riskiest bets, because the smaller the firm and the shorter its track record, the greater is the potential for a few key employee defections (or client losses) to have a devastating impact. Several consulting firms with client bases composed of many startup dot coms, for example, ran into problems in 2000, as venture capital and public market funding for those clients dried up—leaving them unable to pay their consulting bills. Bigger firms probably offer less in the way of growth but more in the way of security. Losing one or two big clients or a handful of senior consultants isn't likely to have as much of an immediate impact on Sapient, with a few thousand employees and annual revenues rapidly approaching a billion dollars, as it is on Diamond Technology Partners, with just a few hundred employees and revenues in the low hundreds of millions. On the other hand, Sapient's white-hot revenue growth is likely to slow gradually, on a percentage basis, as its revenue base gets bigger, while Diamond Technology probably still has a few years of increasing revenue growth ahead of it before that happens.

Sounds simple, right? If you want a lower-risk consulting investment, you go with a bigger firm, if you're willing to take on greater risk, you go with a smaller firm. In a broad sense, that's generally true. But there are exceptions to every rule, which is why it makes sense to refine that selection process just a bit.

First, in a business where morale and employee happiness are so critical, it's worth finding out—from the company directly or from the analysts who cover it—what the company's annual employee turnover rate is. If it's a lot higher than the industry average of 20 percent or 25 percent, that may be a bad sign. Another question worth asking: How did a big firm get so big—and how is a little firm growing so fast? Are these firms growing simply by acquiring other consulting firms? If so, how are they integrating the other firms' employees with their own? In all types of professional services businesses, there's evidence to suggest that mergers and acquisitions aren't the best way to grow—which may be why you see so few law firms or medical practices combining. Cultures are different, personalities clash, and it's just too easy, when there are no hard assets forcing everyone to stay together, for employees to walk out the door. "Companies whose growth is predominantly organic tend to have fundamentally more stable businesses than acquisitive companies," write analysts at Goldman Sachs. "It is easier to do all of the things that good, solid professional services companies need to do: build and foster a single corporate culture, develop consistent project delivery methodologies, have a consistent image for customers, and implement and maintain operational controls." Even assuming those things can be pulled off, Goldman goes so far as to suggest that professional-service acquisitions make little sense on a strictly financial basis. Consider: in past consulting firm mergers, according to Goldman, purchase prices have frequently run to $1 million per employee. Since there's really little in the way of hard assets that come along with that employee, Goldman says, "that's like paying a $1 million fee to a professional recruiter for a new employee whose [total] annual cost to the firm is $125,000 to $140,000 . . . not a bad commission, especially when outside recruiting fees are 20%–30%!"

There are other ways, based on simple numbers, to figure out how well a consulting firm is being run and how important it is to its clients. First, divide the firm's revenues by the number of consultants it employs to come up with revenues per consultant. If a firm is in good health, that number should be at least in the low hundreds of thousands, and it should trend higher over time. A small number, or one that's shrinking, suggests that the firm is either losing business or not being managed efficiently. Second, try to find out, from the firm or from the analysts who cover it, what its average project size is. Project size is a good indicator of how important the consultant is to its clients. That, in turn, is an important indicator of how much future work the consultant is likely to win from that client, or by referral, as well as of how expendable the consultant's services are in the event the client needs to tighten its belt. Goldman suggests that a number in the $4 million and higher range is a good sign. Third, try to determine what portion of a consulting firm's work is from big corporations and what portion is from start-ups—which are likely to spend less per project and to have a tougher time paying their bills. Ideally, a firm should have a mix of both kinds of work: the dependable revenue stream of the big, deep-pocketed clients, along with the new ideas and entrepreneurial spirit that come from working with little guys. Finally, the company's stock price itself is something to consider. Remember: when shopping for a consulting stock, you're not shopping for a cheap stock. A "cheap" consulting stock is a sign of a firm in trouble—and the cheap stock itself can make it harder for the firm to attract top-notch talent. While consultants can rebound from problems, it's difficult. Generally, firms with "buzz" have an easier time attracting smart employees and winning work. And for the most part, their stocks aren't cheap.

MadisonAvenue.com

By this point, it's probably pretty clear that there are basically three ways for Internet companies to make money. They can sell things directly or provide a virtual meeting place where things are sold; they can charge a subscription or membership fee; or they can sell ads. For the average dot com, though, selling ads sounds a lot easier than it actually is. That's especially true in these early days of the Net. For one thing, most Web sites are small, with small audiences and small advertising sales staffs. It's not very obvious what a single moderately trafficked site offers a prospective advertiser—or, for that matter, how an advertiser would find out about the site in the first place. For another thing, advertisers still aren't very comfortable with the idea of paying to advertise on-line. Partly, that's because Internet ads are still pretty boring. They're small—because they have to fit on your computer screen with all sorts of other material—and they're easily ignored. They don't offer the same kinds of visual or aural stimulation that TV or radio ads offer or the kind of space that print ads offer. And advertising agencies, by and large, haven't yet gotten around to offering ads designed for the Net as part of their regular services.

But all that is changing fast. High-speed Internet access is making Web advertising more exciting to look at and listen to. New technologies are allowing advertisers to target ads to specific audiences in a way that traditional print, TV, and radio ads don't. And most important, the Internet is more and more a mainstream phenomenon that advertisers simply can't ignore. Consider these statistics: according to Jupiter Communications, the number of Americans on-line will almost double over the next few years— from 83 million as of the end of 1998 to 157 million by the end of 2003. That's more than half of the entire U.S. population. About half of those users are women—about in line with their percentage in the broader population, and up from about a third just a few years ago. The average income of on-line households is falling, from $62,000 per year in 1998 to an estimated $55,000 by 2003, according to Jupiter—coming closer to the national average of $44,000. The upshot? The Net isn't just for young, rich, nerdy guys anymore.

Once they go on-line, people are spending more and more time there: an average of more than eight hours a week today, according to Jupiter, up from seven a couple of years ago and trending toward ten hours and more a couple of years down the road. That's already more than twice as much time as the average person spends reading newspapers or magazines. And it's closing in on the amount of time spent watching TV or listening to the radio. What's more—to the chagrin of bosses and the delight of advertisers—a lot of that time is during the workday, when employees surf the Web from their office computers. Jupiter even considers Internet "prime time" to be between noon and 4 P.M. That's time that TV, radio, newspaper, and billboard advertisers typically can't get their hands on, because most folks don't watch TV at work, and not many listen to the radio, read the paper, or drive down the highway during those hours. But a lot of folks work on computers at the office—and more and more of them are sneaking in a bit of time to surf the Web.

All in all, it adds up to one gigantic moneymaking opportunity. According to Jupiter, while $151 billion was spent advertising on television, on radio, in print, and on billboards in 1997, just $744 million was spent advertising on-line. But the gap is narrowing fast. On-line advertising is growing at better than 40 percent a year, on average, compared with about 5 percent for the traditional advertising market. Web advertising has already outpaced outdoor advertising in dollars spent annually. And by 2003, Jupiter estimates, companies will spend $11.5 billion advertising on-line, compared with $204 billion off-line. That's close to what they'll spend on cable TV or radio.

There's been some concern, however, that early Web advertising has been dominated by dot coms spending seed capital or IPO money advertising on other dot coms in a sort of giant Ponzi scheme. Another worry: that many dot coms, starved for cash, have paid for the ads they've bought on other sites with "in-kind" services. These barter transactions don't amount to real money spent on Web advertising, though they're recorded as revenues by the companies selling the ad space. All this has unquestionably happened, and it's certainly worth trying to assess how much of a company's business comes from other Internet companies (some companies reveal these data, others don't) and how much of its "sales" are paid for via barter, instead of cash, before investing in it. But overall, Jupiter's research suggests that going forward, the bulk of the money spent advertising on-line will come from traditional firms: media companies, banks and brokerages, car manufacturers, computer and software manufacturers, airlines and hotels, and consumer packaged-goods companies. (Ironically, the bigger impact as many dot coms go out of business could be on traditional advertising agencies and media outlets—TV and radio networks, newspapers and print magazines, and billboards—that will see—and, indeed, are already seeing—a sharp falloff in advertising from Internet companies.)

All this expected advertising largesse is clearly good news for the dot-com companies that'll be on its receiving end. But other than investing in giant Internet media players such as Yahoo! or AOL, which make money in large part by accepting advertising on their sites, how's an Internet investor supposed to take advantage of the trend? The answer: by investing in the Internet advertising networks that act as giant clearinghouses for all those ads. Like real estate agents for ad space, these companies match clients that want to advertise on the Web with other clients that have Web advertising space they want to sell. Just as an investment in a consulting firm is a way of investing in the growth of the Net by proxy, investing in an Internet advertising network is a way of betting on the growth of Internet advertising without putting your money on a single horse who may or may not emerge the winner.

The major players in this space—the biggest is DoubleClick—make money by taking the mystery and hassle out of Internet advertising. They've carved out a giant niche for themselves as the middlemen of Web ads. Advertisers use their services because they need someone to distribute their ads across hundreds of Web sites efficiently, without having to develop relationships and sign separate contracts with each of those sites. Web sites need them even more because the networks' giant sales staffs allow the sites to sell ad space that may otherwise go unfilled. The ad networks, meanwhile, make money by earning a commission every time they place an ad, or—if the deal is performance-based—every time a Web surfer clicks on one of the ads they've placed. Like consulting, this is an inherently profitable business, with gross profit margins north of 50 percent. Think about it: DoubleClick has no inventory or warehouses to maintain, and its biggest expenses are for sales and marketing—essentially, paying a sales staff whose primary purpose is to generate revenue.

But companies like DoubleClick do more than simply match buyers and sellers of advertising space. After all, if that's all they did, their function would ultimately be replaced by the very same advertising agencies and media buyers who now perform those services in the traditional media. Instead, these companies are also technology firms, whose fancy software lets advertisers target their ads in a way that's never been possible in the off-line world. And in advertising, targeting is the name of the game.

First, some background. In the traditional media, targeting is mostly an inexact science that involves a lot of audience profiling and a lot of guessing. A magazine such as *Sports Illustrated*, for example, is likely to feature a lot more ads aimed at a young, athletic, and predominantly male audience than a magazine like *Good Housekeeping*, based on some obvious assumptions about its audience. Those assumptions, in turn, have probably been verified by customer profiles both magazines have compiled over the years. Similarly, television networks use services such as those provided by the AC Nielsen company to measure not just the absolute size of their audiences but also what portions fall within the key demographic ranges that advertisers most covet: men aged eighteen to thirty-four, for example. The networks then base their ad rates on a combination of how big their audience is and how "desirable" it is. Advertisers, in turn, use this information to decide not just how much they're willing to pay but also which network features the audience best suited to their product. CBS, for example, carries a lot more ads for products like Geritol than does the Fox network, because CBS's audience tends to be older.

The Internet allows this kind of targeting to be done in real time. Visit a portal such as Yahoo!, for example, type in the words "fishing tackle," and along with a list of dozens of sites with information about fishing tackle, you'll probably be thrown a few advertisements for businesses that sell fishing tackle. Those businesses pay Yahoo! a premium for that kind of instant targeting, under the (probably correct) assumption that somebody searching for information about fishing tackle is a more likely customer for the product than somebody searching for information on musical instruments. But this kind of targeting, while impressive, only scratches the surface of what's possible.

Company Snapshot: DoubleClick

At a Glance
Ticker symbol: DCLK
Founded: 1996
Went public: 1998
2000 revenue: $506 million
Revenue growth rate (vs. 1999): 96%
2000 losses: $13 million
Profit growth rate (vs. 1999): NA
Key management: Kevin Ryan, CEO

The biggest of the Internet advertising companies, DoubleClick was one of the first companies to develop technology for "serving" advertisements to other Web sites. Though it remains far and away the leader in this business, the company has faced competition from rivals ranging from 24/7 Media to Engage Technologies. Nevertheless—despite a major slowdown in late 2000 and early 2001—the on-line advertising business is ultimately expected to become very large; Goldman Sachs estimates it will grow in excess of 70 percent in 2002, with sales approaching $14 billion.

There are two primary parts to DoubleClick's business: the DART technology side and the advertising network side. DoubleClick's advertising network pairs ad buyers with ad sellers, helping Web sites sell their advertising space and helping advertisers place ads on a network of Web sites. By contrast, DART—which stands for Dynamic Ad Reporting and Targeting—is limited to developing technology that helps advertisers plan and target their on-line advertisements, and that helps Web sites manage their inventory of available advertising space. In addition, DoubleClick owns Abacus, which manages the nation's largest database of off-line names and addresses provided by catalog merchants. Ultimately, DoubleClick hopes to use this massive database to pair consumers' on-line shopping habits with their off-line data, eliminating their anonymity while providing advertisers with much more information about potential customers and a greater ability to target their advertisements. This plan, however, has been the subject of intense scrutiny and criticism from privacy advocates. In the long run, however, the ability to target advertising to specific types of consumers raises the prospect of increasing advertising rates—though in the short run, this hasn't happened, thanks in part to a glut of advertising space available on-line and the ineffective nature of many early Internet advertisements. DoubleClick's fans argue that Internet advertising will become both more popular and more effective once Internet advertisements evolve from the drab and static banner ads that are now standard to more closely resemble the types of commercials currently found on television.

Firms such as DoubleClick and Engage have devised technology that allows them to track Web users from site to site, developing a continuously updated, ever more precise profile of who you are and what you're interested in. Visit a fly-fishing site, for example, and next time you log on—even if it's days later and fly-fishing is no longer on your mind—chances are you'll be thrown ads offering products related to fly-fishing. Or if you develop a track record of visiting sports-related sites, chances are you'll start seeing a lot more ads for sporting goods companies and sports magazines—because ad networks like DoubleClick and Engage "know" that's what you're interested in.

This type of profiling causes advertisers to salivate and privacy advocates to cringe. So far, companies like DoubleClick and Engage claim to have compiled only anonymous profiles—allowing their clients to target Internet users demonstrating particular qualities or interests but not providing the advertisers with personal information about those users, such as their names. In theory, however, marrying names with surfing habits wouldn't be hard to do. DoubleClick, for one, caused a major uproar with its 1999 purchase of Abacus, the country's largest database of off-line catalog shoppers. Abacus has used this data for years to compile mailing lists for direct-mail merchants. But DoubleClick's stated intention was to match that data with its Web-surfer profiles, resulting in highly detailed portraits of millions of Web surfers, complete with their names, addresses, and phone numbers. Such information could be used to track individuals across the Web. While a major public outcry caused DoubleClick to put these plans on hold, the delay is probably only temporary, until things cool down.

Even without matching names with surfing habits, though, the degree of targeting made possible by Internet technology is unprecedented. Its impact is likely to be threefold: it will help make Internet advertising more popular, while at the same time making it more expensive; that, in turn, will benefit sellers of Web advertising; and that, in turn, will benefit the networks that make this ad targeting possible. For now, only a handful of those networks exist. While it's possible that others will spring up offering similar services, the leaders in the space now—such as DoubleClick—have a huge entrenched advantage, including large and growing networks of member sites and growing profiles of Internet users, that'll make it tough for any would-be rivals to catch up.

Summing It All Up

So much for B2B. Besides figuring out what it is several of the major types of B2B companies do, we've also discovered what qualities these companies have in common. Most important, they have highly efficient business models, with minimal inventory or overhead costs and the potential for fat profit margins. They operate in huge potential markets and have the ability to grow their businesses quickly to take advantage of those markets. And their businesses are designed to become more profitable the bigger they get, though this is more true of the trade exchanges than it is of the consultants and advertising networks. All in all, this adds up to powerful business models and good opportunities for investors.

But these companies are also very different from one another in key respects, including who their clients are and how vital their services are to those clients. Chances are the industrial giants who participate in VerticalNet's various trade exchanges, for example, aren't the same companies who are targeting consumers with banner ads on DoubleClick's advertising network. At the same time, those industrial giants are likely to be far more dependent on the business they transact over that trade exchange than DoubleClick's advertisers are on their banner ads. Advertising, after all, is usually one of the first line items to shrink when corporate belts are tightened, while the raw materials used in manufacturing processes are far less discretionary. Does that make VerticalNet a safer investment than DoubleClick? Not necessarily. DoubleClick, after all, probably has many more clients than VerticalNet, so its revenues are more diverse, though its competition for those clients is probably also more intense.

What this boils down to, then, is that B2B investors shouldn't necessarily pick an investment or two and consider themselves finished with the sector. Compared with the consumer-oriented companies studied in Chapter Three, the B2B sector is broader and more complex. While an investor may put money behind eBay and Yahoo! and be done with the consumer stocks—having covered the two key bases of commerce and advertising—a similar approach in B2B will leave bases uncovered and opportunities on the table. In short, the convergence we found among consumer companies—where the distinctions between commerce, content, and community have blurred—doesn't really exist in B2B. The markets served by the trade exchanges, advertising networks, and consulting firms that are components of the B2B subsector are distinct from one another, and investments in these categories are not interchangable. What's more, in the next chapter, I'll explore an even broader array of companies that do business with other companies—the infrastructure vendors—which will open up the array of investment opportunities even further.

CHAPTER FIVE

Servers and Switches and Routers, Oh My!

Building the Internet's Backbone

Wʜᴀᴛ ɪꜱ ᴛʜᴇ Iɴᴛᴇʀɴᴇᴛ?

In one sense, of course, the Net is a purely virtual medium—fleeting compositions of flickering electrons that crash against your computer screen and are gone in an instant. At the same time, the Net is about as physical a medium as there is. The orders that send those electrons on their kamikaze runs originate from tiny circuits etched on silicon chips housed in big computers in faraway locations. Those orders then travel, by photon or electron, across miles of glass or copper cables, guided by machines called switches and routers, to your computer, where more circuits on other chips translate them back into the electrons that crash into your screen, creating those illusory images. The electrons disappear instantly. (Even the companies behind them may not last!) But those circuits and chips and switches and routers and miles upon miles of cable aren't so ephemeral. They are the Internet's physical backbone. And just as you can invest in the dot-com companies that most people think of when they think of the Net, you can also invest in the builders of that physical infrastructure without which those virtual companies couldn't exist.

There are thousands of different parts of that physical backbone, and as a result there are many kinds of infrastructure companies. There are the companies such as Intel and Advanced Micro Devices that make the microprocessors, or "chips," that power your desktop computer or the big "server" computer in that faraway location that actually houses in the dark recesses of its memory the Web sites you like to visit. For our purposes, we won't consider those chip companies to be Internet companies, because even though the Internet requires those chips to exist, the chips do all sorts of other things as well (such as allowing you to run your word processor, your spreadsheet program, and so on). The Internet isn't their primary or exclusive focus. (These companies do, however, benefit from the Net, so we'll consider them in the next chapter, which examines exactly those kinds of companies.) In the same way, the Net depends on phone lines, cable lines, and electrical power, but the companies that create all those things aren't strictly Internet companies either, even though their businesses certainly benefit from the Net (more on that later, as well).

The Net is, however, a primary focus of companies like Sun Microsystems that make the big "server" computers that power all those Web sites, as well as of companies such as Exodus Communications and AboveNet Communications that operate "server farms"—secure facilities that house servers in a controlled environment. The Net is also a primary focus of companies such as Cisco Systems that create the machines known as "switches" and "routers" that steer Internet traffic around the phone and cable networks, as well as companies such as Inktomi and Akamai Technologies that develop technology to help speed the flow of that traffic, essentially preventing traffic jams. The Internet is the focus of software makers such as VeriSign and Entrust Technologies that create programs allowing for the secure conduct of commerce and communications across the Net. And the Net is most certainly the focus of companies such as AOL, Excite@Home, NetZero, PSINet, and Verio (now a subsidiary of Japan's NTT Communications) that allow individuals or businesses to send and receive data across those Cisco routers to and from those Sun servers. All these companies, in one way or another, are builders of the Internet's physical infrastructure.

A Touchy-Feely Kind of Company

In one sense, Internet infrastructure companies are among the safest of dot-com investments because, unlike their virtual counterparts, they actually *make* something. In that way, a company like Cisco is easier to get your arms around than a company like Yahoo!, because you can literally get your arms around its products! You can touch and feel a Cisco switch or router, and while you may not grasp the mechanics of how it operates, it's obvious that there's something there. Not so for Yahoo!, which is as virtual a company as there is. Sure, Yahoo! has offices where lots of employees sit in cubicles, working at computers. But its only true *assets*, if you can call them that, are the servers sitting in a warehouse, sending and receiving data. Yahoo! doesn't actually *make* anything.

Another benefit of infrastructure companies is that they are, to some degree, an agnostic form of investment. Sure, Cisco has competitors, such as Lucent Technologies, Nortel Networks, and Juniper Networks, to which it might lose business. But on the whole, all those companies should benefit as traffic on the Internet grows, creating more demand for switches, routers, and other products. Again, not so for Yahoo!, which may or may not benefit from that traffic, depending on its ability to convince Internet users to come to its Web site. The growth of the Internet as a whole doesn't *necessarily* create more demand for Yahoo!, as it does for Cisco, Lucent, Nortel, and Juniper.

A third benefit of infrastructure companies is that the barriers to entry in the business are relatively high. One of the biggest problems confronting many Internet business models is that anybody can create a Web site and set up shop as a dot com. Not all those businesses will succeed; in fact, most won't. But they can still do damage to existing businesses by undercutting them on prices or requiring them to invest more heavily in marketing while they're around. That's less true in the infrastructure business, where setting up operations takes more than just a good idea. To represent a credible presence in the infrastructure sector requires both a considerable amount of technical know-how and a sizable investment to bring that idea into production. As we'll see later on, one of the biggest reasons Cisco has been such a phenomenally successful company is its sheer size and financial firepower, as well as the depth of its customer relationships. While would-be competitors are springing up with improved technologies all the time, it's a tough prospect for them to muscle in on Cisco's territory. Far easier, in many cases, is for them simply to sell out to Cisco, which is what dozens of companies have done in recent years, becoming part of Cisco's family of products, rather than challenging the entrenched giant head-on.

That's not to say such competitive threats don't exist. They absolutely do. In fact, one of the biggest downside risks to investing in infrastructure companies is that their technology will become obsolete. Cisco, for example, may have been able to swallow up many of its would-be rivals over the years, but it hasn't gotten them all. Upstart Juniper, for example—which wasn't around just a few years ago—now owns technology that poses a serious threat to Cisco in at least a few product areas. What's more, as investors, it's difficult for us to figure out which company's technology is superior and stands the better chance of succeeding until that's already happened. The reason, of course, is that it's tough for us to really know what it is these companies do. If a fundamental principle of investing is to know what you're buying, infrastructure companies aren't exactly the most obvious of investments, because even though we can touch and feel their products, those products aren't so easy to understand. As Peter Lynch puts it, "Gig my gigahertz and whetstone my megaflop, if you couldn't tell if that was a racehorse or a memory chip you should stay away from it, even though your broker will be calling to recommend it as the opportunity of the decade to make countless nanobucks."

On the other hand, while avoiding the hard-to-understand names is a safe strategy, it's also one that can lead to a lot of missed opportunities. As it happens, I know more than a few grandmothers—conservative investors all—who are thanking their lucky stars their brokers convinced them to buy and hold on to Cisco Systems through the 1990s, even though they haven't the foggiest idea what Cisco Systems does. Does that mean I'd recommend a strategy of investing in companies you don't understand simply because their stocks seem hot (or, Heaven forbid, simply because your broker recommended them)? Heck, no. But if you're prepared to do a little homework, the fact is that Internet infrastructure companies aren't so complicated to understand, at least not at their most basic level. And that's really all you need. You don't need to be an MIT-educated computer scientist and you don't need to understand the finer details of dense wave division multiplexing to pick a winning stock. If you understand the basics and you know what to look for in terms of key measures of performance, you can make some educated guesses about which infrastructure companies may be worth putting your money into, and which are best avoided. Which brings us to an obvious question . . .

What the Heck Is a Router, Anyway?

We've established that the Internet is a network of computers all around the world that talk to one another. At its most basic level, this sprawling network is focused around hubs of giant storage computers, which are essentially massive memory banks, and more complex computers, called "servers," which actually interact with the Net's millions of users. The machines work in tandem, archiving and "serving up" the information that constitutes the Web. Electronic communications among this array of computers—from servers to desktop PCs—are carried along miles of cable, or increasingly, transmitted through the air on radio waves. How do those data transmissions know how to get from point A to point B? And once they get there, how does computer B understand and interpret the message from computer A? That's where devices known as switches and routers come into play.

Much of the modern Internet's physical infrastructure was invented at Stanford University in the early 1980s. It was there that a young German computer scientist, Andy Bechtolsheim, sought to create a powerful computer with many times the memory capacity of a standard desktop that would share computing power across a network of smaller desktop terminals, or workstations. The concept behind this machine—that "the network *is* the computer"—became the premise of a company Bechtolsheim went on to create with three partners. That firm, Sun Microsystems—the name derives from *Stanford University Network*—today dominates the market for network computers.

Around the same time, two Stanford computer scientists, Len Bosack and Sandy Lerner, a married couple, grew frustrated over the fact that the computers in Len's department couldn't send and receive e-mail from the computers in Sandy's department. Len's computers could communicate with one another, exchanging information over cables that connected them in what's called a "local area network." And Sandy's computers could communicate with one another in the same way. But the two computer networks didn't speak the same language. They couldn't be tied together because, quite literally, they wouldn't be able to understand each other. Setting about to solve this dilemma, the two computer scientists invented the "router," a machine that analyzes and translates data and steers it among computer networks, figuring out the best way to "route" it from its origin to its destination. (Technically, the first router had been invented some years earlier by scientists working on the first computer network, the ARPANET, discussed in Chapter One. But Bosack and Lerner are generally credited with developing the first commercially viable router—smaller, more practical to use, and broader in its applications.) The device allowed Len's little network to talk to Sandy's little network—and ultimately many other networks, creating "internetwork" communications. (Now you see where the term "Internet" comes from.) The development created a stir not just at Stanford but in computer science departments across the country, many of which wanted to buy one. When Stanford refused to give their budding business its blessing, Bosack and Lerner set out on their own, ultimately winning the financial backing to create a new company in their living room: Cisco Systems (the name derives from San Francisco). Today, Cisco controls well over three quarters of the router market, and the company proudly boasts that 90 percent of Internet traffic flows over its devices.

A bit later came the development of the "switch," a less expensive machine that performs many of the same functions as the router but on a smaller scale, and faster. While routers are mostly used by major Internet service providers and telecommunications companies to translate and steer huge amounts of traffic among a vast array of computer and server networks, switches are used for smaller jobs within corporate or university networks (intranets, as opposed to the Internet). They're mostly used for translating and relaying information along frequently used pathways and don't need to calculate complicated routes among various networks. Originally, Cisco wasn't in the switching business, and it saw switches as a potential threat to its routers. After all, routers do what switches do and more, so why not sell a customer a high-priced router instead of a lower-priced switch? Ultimately, though, Cisco realized that, like it or not, its customers were buying switches for their smaller jobs. And the company came to the conclusion that it would lose more business by refusing to manufacture switches than it would cannibalize from its existing router sales by getting into the switching business. The result: it bought a switching company, ultimately coming to dominate the switch-making business in the same way it dominates the router business and embarking on what would become an extraordinarily successful strategy of snapping up competing new technologies before they have a chance to inflict too much damage.

Two Pigs in a Poke?
A Look at Sun Versus Cisco

Though their businesses are very different, both Sun and Cisco dominate their respective spaces, and both are frequently considered cornerstones of any winning technology investment portfolio. Roughly the same age, the companies have both grown rapidly, and both continue to benefit from the explosive growth of the Internet. Both companies boast fat gross profit margins—in excess of 50 percent for Sun, north of 60 percent for Cisco—and eye-popping revenue growth rates—topping 20 percent annually for Sun and 50 percent annually for Cisco (though in Cisco's case, that number is widely expected to moderate quite a bit in the next few years). But in terms of management style and competitive threats, key factors for investors to consider, the similarities end there. Because of this, and because of how prominent they are in the Internet infrastructure business, they're worth examining a little more closely.

Sun's management, currently presided over by the feisty and sharp-tongued Scott McNealy, is focused mostly on "organic" growth—a fancy Wall Street term for growth from within rather than through acquisition. Partly, this is a function of the competitive environment in which Sun operates. Sun's servers use an operating system known as UNIX—a computer language favored by many software programmers because, among other things, it is "open-source," meaning that programmers can manipulate the core "DNA" of the code relatively easily, according to their needs. UNIX is also reliable, meaning that UNIX-based programs tend to "crash" less frequently than other programs when performing complicated tasks. UNIX's competition is primarily the Windows NT operating system created by Microsoft. That system is "proprietary," meaning that Microsoft controls the source code. It's also generally considered less stable than UNIX, though recent upgrades may change that. But NT has been able to gain ground at least partly because of Microsoft's industry clout. (This explains the fierce rivalry between Sun and Microsoft and, more specifically, between Sun's McNealy and Microsoft Chairman Bill Gates and CEO Steve Ballmer.) More recently, UNIX has faced competition as well from a newer upstart operating system called Linux, which is similar to UNIX but can be even more easily manipulated by programmers. Linux, however, is less powerful. It tends to work better on smaller-scale systems than on the most powerful servers made by Sun, and competition between Sun and the upstart makers of Linux-powered machines has, so far at least, been less intense.

As a result of these different types of operating systems, though, Sun has two kinds of competitors in the server business. On the one hand, it faces traditional rivals such as Hewlett-Packard and IBM, both of which have made high-end NT- and UNIX-powered servers and both of which have tried, with relatively little success, to chip away at Sun's market share (though H-P has recently scored a number of high-profile contract wins that may indicate it is gaining traction). Part of the problem these companies face is high barriers to entry, which applies even to giants such as H-P and IBM. Sun was essentially the creator of the network computer, and it simply dominates the market.

On the other hand, Sun also faces newer competition at the low end from companies such as VA Linux Systems and Network Appliance, which manufacture the less powerful systems—often Linux-based—that are used in corporate or university intranets but not generally on the Internet itself. But these are lower-margin products, and these companies are still small enough that, so far at least, they pose little threat to Sun. Given this competitive landscape—and its own phenomenal growth and market share—Sun has had little reason or opportunity to merge with or acquire any of its rivals.

Cisco, by contrast, has acquired other companies at breakneck speed. In its case, that too has been a function of market conditions. As we've seen, Cisco departed from its original business of manufacturing routers used for handling large volumes of data traffic only when it learned that some customers were choosing to buy lower-priced switches to handle smaller volumes of data within smaller computer networks. Essentially, these firms were saying they didn't need to buy a V-8 Cadillac when a four-cylinder Chevy would do the job. It wasn't that they didn't *want* to do business with Cisco; on the contrary, one of Cisco's claims to fame is its legendary attention to customer service. The problem was, Cisco didn't make switches and would have required considerable time and money to figure out how to make them as well as or better than the companies that already did. So Cisco's management, overruling concerns among the firm's router sales force that selling switches would kill their business, went out and bought a switch maker. In one fell swoop, the company gained a technology and a manufacturing process it lacked, along with some new clients—and avoided the risk of having its own technology made obsolete.

The experiment worked. Cisco found that by acquiring rivals, it was able to serve existing customers better, offering them a range of products they couldn't find anyplace else. As the technology for switches and routers has continued to evolve at warp speed, Cisco has followed along, gobbling up little companies at the forefront of that technology. Of course, like Sun, Cisco has deep-pocketed rivals to worry about—names such as Nortel, Lucent, and Newbridge Networks, which are increasingly copying its successful strategy. But many analysts, and Cisco executives too, believe the bigger threat to the company's continued dominance comes from unknown up-starts, who in a single stroke can develop new technology that makes Cisco's products seem old-fashioned. Juniper Networks, for exam-ple, developed a high-speed router that, for a time, was significantly faster than anything Cisco offered, helping it eat into Cisco's busi-ness at the very high end. Partly, the differences in the competitive situation between Sun and Cisco are a function of the fact that the technology for transporting data has changed and developed at a faster rate than the technology for storing and serving up those data. What's more, different sizes and types of networks—copper, cable, fiber optic—require different kinds of switches and routers. As each of these technologies has developed, Cisco has bought a company that provides it. For example, having come of age largely in the era of less robust corporate intranets and copper networks, Cisco has had to scramble to play catch-up with companies like Juniper, whose ex-clusive focus has been to develop products for the glass-based, fiber-optic networks that are increasingly being rolled out to carry enormous volumes of Internet traffic. In just the past couple of years, Cisco has spent billions of dollars scooping up makers of ad-vanced optical networking equipment designed for these glass-based networks. And the company has become a magnet for deals as many tiny, upstart companies have found that selling out to Cisco early is a safer, easier alternative to an iffy and protracted effort to take the networking giant on head-to-head as a competitor.

While growth through acquisition is often considered sus-pect—integrating companies can be difficult and lead to all sorts of accounting and personnel nightmares—Cisco has pulled off its string of deals with what seems like spectacular ease. Partly, that's because it has been acquiring companies a fraction of its own size, which are easier to integrate. Partly, also, it's because Cisco's man-agement has worked hard to integrate acquisitions and make new employees feel like members of the Cisco family. Buying a high-technology company for a few billion dollars can be a waste if its most valuable assets—smart people—walk out the door the minute the deal is done. The fact that Cisco's stock has been a stellar per-former hasn't hurt either, providing an incentive for newly acquired employees to stay with the company and providing Cisco with the currency it needs to keep doing deals.

There is a flip side to all this, which is the added risk that comes from growing via acquisition. Should Cisco stumble, its highly valued stock is likely to take a particularly brutal pounding from investors, who have shown little tolerance for slowing revenue growth or missed earnings targets. In that case, Cisco's problems would almost certainly have a domino effect, making it more expensive for it to buy other firms, tougher to keep employee morale high, and, as a result, tougher to hold on to employees and integrate acquired companies. And even absent a decline in its stock price, Cisco's strategy of gobbling up its rivals isn't foolproof. Occasionally, a potential rival comes along that doesn't show up on Cisco's radar screen until late in the game or that doesn't want to sell. Consider Juniper or another firm, Redback Networks, that makes specialized high-performance switches. So far, this hasn't been a problem. But too many such rivals could start to nibble away at Cisco's market share in a more serious way.

An Elephant Never Forgets

Besides servers, switches, and routers, storage computers function as yet another piece of the Internet infrastructure puzzle. In terms of what they do, they're decidedly less glamorous. Like lumbering elephants, they are essentially giant disk drives that serve as the Internet's memory banks. But as stocks, the companies that make them have been anything but lumbering. One storage company, EMC, was the single best-performing stock on the New York Stock Exchange during the 1990s. If Cisco rules the roost when it comes to switches and routers and Sun is king when it comes to servers, then it is EMC and another firm, Network Appliance, that are the grandaddies of the storage business. They, too, have serious competitors. Sun, Dell Computer, IBM, Hewlett-Packard, and Compaq Computer Corporation are all players in the storage game, often selling storage devices as part of a package, along with their servers. But EMC and Network Appliance are pure-play storage companies, selling storage devices that can be added onto existing setups as memory banks inevitably fill up.

Theirs is not a terribly complicated business, but it's growing at lightning speed. Think about it: the Internet has resulted in an explosion of data. Already, there are an estimated 1 billion Web pages in existence, and that number is growing by leaps and bounds. International Data Corporation estimates that the annual growth rate is 70 percent, suggesting that the total number of documents on the Web will top 13 billion by 2003. Indeed, other studies indicate that at any given time, as many as 20 percent of the Web pages in existence have been created within the previous *two weeks.* Every time you log on, you're creating more data—information about where you surf that's being stored and analyzed by advertising companies, shopping records that are being archived by the vendors that sell you goods and services, messages that are posted on message boards and in chat rooms. Where does all that information go? Onto storage computers, where it gets filed away. According to estimates by Goldman Sachs, the market for storage computers will easily double over the next several years, translating into annual revenue growth in excess of 20 percent for the industry, as well as for its leading players. Overall, Goldman estimates that the storage market will hit $50 billion by 2003. And it is quite profitable, with operating profit margins of 20 percent to 25 percent.

As in the server, switch, and router businesses, the storage business is segmented into a high end, a middle range, and a low end—depending on a system's requirements—and different companies dominate different parts of the business. EMC, for example, is the leader in building the biggest storage devices—those containing one *tera*byte or more of memory, or enough to store 700 million printed pages of information, and able to interact with both UNIX and NT servers. Other players here include IBM, Hewlett-Packard, Sun, and StorageTek. EMC is also now the leader in midrange storage devices—which have less than one terabyte worth of memory but can interact with multiple operating systems—since its acquisition of a company called Data General that was the leader in that space. At the lower end, dominating the so-called server-attached storage space, are Sun and Compaq, which have parlayed their big server businesses into sales of storage computers that attach to a single server dedicated to those storage devices and operate on just one operating system. Finally, there are the so-called network-attached storage devices, which connect not to one server, but to multiple servers on an intranet or local area network. Network Appliance controls about 40 percent of this market, with a company called Auspex Systems in second place at about 20 percent market share.

One recent innovation in the storage business has been the development of what are called "storage area networks," or SANs. A SAN is a group of servers and storage devices that are interconnected, so that any server can access any storage device (rather than having storage devices connected to specific servers). As a result, they offer increased speed and flexibility. They are also tricky to develop, and whole companies have sprung up largely to create the hardware and software needed to get all these servers and storage devices to talk to one another. Among the leaders in storage software are companies such as Veritas Software and Legato Systems, while companies such as Brocade Communications Systems and Gadzoox Networks develop specialized switches for these mininetworks.

Indeed, within the storage business, the storage software business is an interesting niche. While companies such as EMC do develop their own software, companies such as Veritas and Legato also offer software that helps manage storage devices: moving data around, copying it, and controlling access to it. According to Dataquest, the storage software business is growing at a rate of 21 percent a year and will hit $6.6 billion by 2003. Goldman Sachs suggests that the growth rate is likely to be even faster. What's more, software is a more profitable part of the business. Goldman estimates that it carries operating profit margins of between 40 and 45 percent, close to twice that of the hardware side of the business.

Piggyback Businesses

As we've seen, servers, storage computers, switches, and routers are four of the key components of the Internet's physical backbone, the first two acting together to archive and dish up the reams of information that flow across the Net, the second two helping to steer that flow of data and ease communications among the various machines. With the growth of the Net, however, whole companies have sprung up whose business models piggyback on the server-storage-switch-router backbone. Among them: companies such as Exodus and AboveNet, whose entire business centers around operating giant "server farms," specially constructed facilities designed to safeguard servers in optimum environments. Housed in secure buildings kept under twenty-four-hour lock and key, these facilities feature insulated, earthquake-proof floors, specialized air-conditioning systems, fire-suppression systems, redundant electrical supplies, and hundreds of high-speed telecommunications lines from multiple Internet service providers. The idea: to take much of the physical concern associated with operating a Web site off the hands of the Web site operator, ensuring that so-called mission-critical operations—those that are the lifeblood of a business and without which it couldn't function—are secure. Rather than spend considerable sums to build and maintain the redundant systems needed to ensure utility-like stability for their core computer systems, for example, companies such as eBay or Amazon can simply outsource these responsibilities to a specialist, at an average cost of about $200,000 per year.

Fans of these companies contend that they are fast-growing, high-margin businesses—that with little in the way of initial investment, they will profit directly from the growth of the Net as more and more companies open Web sites and need a place to maintain their servers. According to Forrester Research, the Web hosting business will hit annual revenues of $42 billion by the year 2003, up from just over $10 billion in the year 2000. Exodus, currently the leader in the business, with millions of square feet of server-farm space in operation or under construction, is expected to have long-term gross profit margins approaching 40 percent or more.

Critics retort that there is little real need for these types of firms—that as the Web becomes more of an ingrained feature of life and technologies grow more sophisticated, there'll be little need for a place whose only purpose is to put a roof over a server's head. That, they say, is something more and more companies will just do on their own—or that will be provided as part of a broader set of products, along with things such as phone service. While it's too early to know for sure, it does seem likely that server-farm companies won't survive forever in their current, single-focus form. Already, for example, Japan's largest phone company, NTT Communications, has acquired Verio, a big player in the Web hosting business, and companies ranging from Intel to AT&T to WorldCom to Verizon have entered the Web hosting business on their own. Many of these firms may seek to gobble up leading Web hosting providers. Meanwhile, the Web hosting companies themselves are beginning to branch out into highly profitable side businesses, such as Web site monitoring and security, in an effort to diversify their revenues and become ever more critical to their clients.

Company Snapshot: Exodus Communications

At a Glance
Ticker symbol: EXDS
Founded: 1994
Went public: 1998
2000 revenue: $818.4 million
Revenue growth rate (vs. 1999): 238%
2000 losses: $221.5 million
Profit growth rate (vs. 1999): NA
Key management: Ellen Hancock, Chairman and CEO

The largest of the so-called Web hosting companies, Exodus is a high-end hotel of sorts for the often fragile technology that is at the heart of the World Wide Web. The company operates dozens of specially designed data centers around the world, each of which offers tight physical security, reinforced floors, redundant electrical supplies, ultraprecise climate control systems, and other features necessary for the safe care and housing of the servers and storage devices on which thousands of Web sites are housed. Exodus's clients include not only hundreds of dot coms but also many bricks-and-mortar companies that don't want to build—or don't have the resources to build—such premium facilities to house their computer servers.

Exodus's revenues come primarily from the rent it charges for its real estate. But the company also derives fees from other services it provides, including Web site monitoring, helping to ensure that its clients' Web sites are up and running at all times.

Though it is the largest player in its field, Exodus does face competition, including potentially from telecom giants such as WorldCom and AT&T that are hungrily eyeing its business. So far, though, the company has managed to carve out a healthy and lucrative niche for itself, and its business continues to grow by leaps and bounds. In 2000, the company acquired one of its largest competitors, the GlobalCenter unit of Global Crossing. Global Crossing is now Exodus's largest shareholder and has an exclusive long-term arrangement with the company to be its premier provider of telecommunications services.

A model similar to the server-hosting business is that of storage-capacity providers, which rent out space on storage computers to other companies that need them. Rather than go out and buy a whole storage system for your small business, for example, you could more cheaply rent as much space as you need from a storage-capacity provider, paying that vendor just as you would your electric or water utility, on an as-used basis. Much as companies in the software space, known as applications service providers, rent out software and services, storage-capacity providers allow businesses to avoid making massive up-front investments in computer systems that are bigger than they might ever need (or at least might need for quite some time). One leading player in this space is a company called StorageNetworks. While it has a smart and highly profitable business model, one conceivable threat to this business is that it could be displaced by the storage vendors themselves, should they decide to simply rent out space on their own systems. For now, though, that hasn't happened, and companies such as StorageNetworks have succeeded in carving out a nice niche for themselves as technology landlords.

Company Snapshot: Akamai Technologies

At a Glance
Ticker symbol: AKAM
Founded: 1998
Went public: 1999
2000 revenue: $89.8 million
Revenue growth rate (vs. 1999): 2152%
2000 losses: $182.2 million
Profit growth rate (vs. 1999): NA
Key management: George Conrades, Chairman and CEO

Like its cross-country rival Inktomi, Akamai, based in Cambridge, Massachusetts, develops technology for speeding the delivery of Internet content. Though not identical, the software operates in a similar fashion, storing multiple copies of the most sought-after content on multiple, geographically dispersed computer servers and steering requests for that content to the server located closest to the user. This dispersing of information and information requests to a network of servers sitting around the Web's "edge" reduces the frequency of data traffic jams at the Web's more congested center.

Akamai has developed a clever marketing campaign for its service, referring to Web sites that use its technology as "Akamaized" sites. And the company has a number of big clients, from Lands' End to Microsoft to Reuters. But unlike Inktomi, Akamai is a company much more focused on its core, content-delivery business. That can be a good thing, if it is able to become the undisputed leader in that business and grow its market share. On the other hand, investors should keep in mind that Akamai does one thing and one thing only—which may make it a somewhat risky bet, as well.

A third business model that has piggybacked off the server-storage-switch-router infrastructure is that of the so-called caching or content distribution firms. These companies, such as Inktomi and Akamai Technologies, create hardware and software that also help speed the flow of information around the Internet by storing it in multiple locations (these locations are called "caches," pronounced "cashes," and the process is called "caching"). The theory is that for frequently requested data, centralizing access through a single server guarantees a traffic bottleneck. Even if routers are able to ensure that requests for that information are speedily directed to the appropriate server—and that the information itself is speedily routed back—the ability to access the data is constrained by the many requests bombarding the same server at the same time. What's more, the mere act of routing data and data requests over long distances takes time, sucks up capacity on the Internet backbone, and, as a result, costs Internet service providers money in the form of telecommunications expenses (remember: you might pay a flat fee for unlimited Internet service, but the more time you spend on-line and the more bandwidth you consume, the more money your Internet service provider has to cough up to its telecommunications provider). Inktomi and Akamai have devised similar ways of dealing with this problem, by copying "hot" data into multiple, geographically separate hubs, so that requests for that information will be directed to the hub closest to the request. *Bingo!* Your ISP saves money because the request is served faster and consumes less long-distance bandwidth, the Web site you dialed up is happy because its servers aren't being clogged by too many requests for the same information, and you're happy because the Web page you requested takes less time to download.

Already important, caching is becoming more so as the number of people on-line increases and the Net becomes more and more congested. By some estimates, demand for bandwidth—essentially, space on the "pipes" that carry Internet content—is doubling every six months, far faster than new bandwidth is being built. In its mildest form, this increasing congestion causes Web pages to download slowly, often agonizingly so. In its worst form, it causes Web sites to be totally inaccessible. The problem is compounded by the fact that people tend to go on-line at the same time and to access the same information, including special events such as the Web cast of the Victoria's Secret fashion show or the posting of the Starr Report on President Clinton. And the situation is expected to get worse as Web content evolves from its current form—generally static combinations of text and images—to include more and more "rich media," with audio and video content that looks like television.

This is all good news for caching and content-distribution companies, because it means a greater need for their products for the foreseeable future. And since caching is largely a software business, it is highly profitable. Inktomi, currently a leader in the space, carries gross profit margins in the mid–80 percent range. Eventually, though, it's a good bet that these profit margins will shrink. At some point, perhaps years from now, it stands to reason that bandwidth will catch up to demand, presumably making caching products less valuable and more like commodities.

Company Snapshot: Inktomi

At a Glance
Ticker symbol: INKT
Founded: 1996
Went public: 1999
Fiscal 2000 revenue: $223.5 million (year ended Sept. 30)
Revenue growth rate (vs. 1999): 204%
Fiscal 2000 profits: $13 million (year ended Sept. 30)
Profit growth rate (vs. 1999): NA
Key management: David Peterschmidt, President and CEO

Though the name "Inktomi" (pronounced "INK-to-me") might seem bizarre, the term—a Lakota Indian word for a clever spider—is actually a reference to Inktomi's core software, which was one of the Internet's first search engines. This software, built around a complex series of algorithms, "crawls" around the World

Wide Web, searching for specific terms. Like InfoSpace, Inktomi has adopted a strategy of remaining essentially unbranded as far as consumers are concerned, allowing it to sell its technology to multiple companies who are one anothers' rivals. Thus, Inktomi's search engine was, for a long time, used by all three of the biggest Internet portal sites—Yahoo!, AOL, and MSN—though most users of those sites probably had no idea they were using the exact same software.

More recently, Inktomi has faced intense competition in the search engine space, as rivals from AltaVista to Google to Northern Light Technology (all privately held) have come up with their own technologies that perform the same function. Indeed, in 2000, Inktomi lost its primary Yahoo! account to Google, though it picked up a new piece of Yahoo!'s business, powering the search engines for portals Yahoo! custom-builds for corporate clients.

Meanwhile, Inktomi has diversified its businesses, developing software to speed the delivery of Web site content. Inktomi's caching (pronounced "cashing") technology is now widely used by Internet companies to help their sites function better and more quickly. The software works by storing copies of the most frequently requested Web content on multiple computer servers and then routing requests for that content to the server located closest to the user. The process helps control the flood of information requests to a single server that can bring a Web site crashing down. But Inktomi also faces rather intense competition in this space, including from Akamai, which offers a similar content-delivery technology.

I Want My ISP

Most of the Internet infrastructure we've talked about so far is totally invisible to us. In fact, the vast majority of Web surfers will probably go through life having been touched by routers and caching software millions of times without ever knowing it. In the same way, we all use toilets, but few of us know many details about the mechanics of the toilet's plumbing, or for that matter about the inside of the sewer system. That said, most people probably know that their toilet is linked to the sewer system, and they know that if they stop paying their water bill, the toilet will stop working. Similarly, even if we don't know exactly how switches and routers steer our data traffic across the pipes of the telecommunications network, to and from servers all around the world, we do know that to link up to that telecommunications infrastructure, we need to have an Internet service provider (ISP), such as America Online, Excite@Home, EarthLink, or NetZero. These companies are the most obvious points of contact between the Internet and its users, and as such, they are probably the best-known infrastructure firms.

There are two types of ISPs: the dial-up kind, also known as "narrowband," and the always-on kind, also known as "broadband." Eventually, all Internet service will probably be broadband, and the Internet will always be "on," just as the electricity is always on in your house and accessing it requires simply flipping a switch. For now, though, most people have dial-up Internet service at home and always-on Internet service at work. Dial-up service transmits data to and from your Internet service provider over standard copper phone lines; every time you want to connect to the Internet, you dial up a local access number to your Internet service provider, and a series of strange, fax-machine-like noises emanates from your computer as it sends and receives data over those lines to the router at your ISP's local office. Dial-up, narrowband service is typically quite slow, because it's sharing those copper phone lines with all sorts of other data and voice signals, and it's prone to crashing, because those "narrow" copper phone lines weren't designed to carry that kind of traffic. Broadband service—transmitted over cable lines, fiber-optic lines, or so-called digital subcriber lines (essentially, regular copper phone lines with upgraded connections at both ends)—is faster, and it's often referred to as "high-speed" Internet service. Cable, fiber-optic, and DSL lines are all "fatter pipes" than traditional phone lines, which is why they're called *broadband*. That doesn't mean the cables are necessarily thicker—though they often are—but that each of those cables has much greater capacity and is capable of carrying far more data traffic, at higher speeds, than the old copper phone lines can (fiber-optic lines, for example, transmit information using light pulses rather than electricity). Broadband service doesn't require you to dial it up every time you want to access it; just as your cable TV service is always there when you switch it on, broadband Internet service is always there when you click on the Internet browser icon on your computer.

Essentially, what your ISP does is provide you with an on-ramp to the Internet. Just as your local phone company offers you access to the telephone system and your local electric utility offers you access to the electrical grid, your ISP simply offers you a connection to the Internet's "backbone"—the very fat pipes that connect server computers, via routers, around the world (those pipes don't connect directly to desktop computers, just as electrical lines go through a series of transformers before they connect to your outlet). Many ISPs supplement this on-ramp service with additional services, such as free e-mail and a portal site that is the first thing you see when you log on and that provides you with a search engine and a mix of content and shopping options (recall our discussion of portals in Chapter Three). But these services are really incidental to the ISP's primary function; they're a way of winning your loyalty and of milking additional revenue out of you, either by throwing advertising at you or by getting you to spend money buying things from your ISP and its partners. America Online, the nation's largest ISP, has taken this multiple-revenue-stream model to the extreme. Though it started out as simply one of hundreds of services that offered users a connection to the Internet, AOL directed tremendous resources and energy at becoming a premier portal site, offering its own content and content aggregated from other providers to its users. As we saw in Chapter Two, its acquisition of Time Warner has made it one of the world's largest media and content companies, providing the company with reams upon reams of brand-name off-line content that it can translate into on-line content. (The Time Warner deal also gives AOL ownership of the nation's second largest cable company, and with it direct control over a major broadband pipe into millions of homes.)

Most ISPs make money through monthly access fees charged to subscribers, through advertising and commerce, or through both. Broadband services, such as Excite@Home and Road Runner, typically charge the most, $40 or $50 a month. Narrowband services, meanwhile, come in several tiers. Some, such as America Online, EarthLink, and MSN, have branded themselves as "premium" services. They charge the highest fees—in the mid-$20 range, per month—in exchange for the promise of more user-friendly features. Others, such as CompuServe (a unit of AOL), target a more cost-conscious audience with a "value" service that costs less but offers fewer amenities. Still others, such as NetZero, offer Internet access free of charge in exchange for users agreeing to fill out comprehensive questionnaires about their background, income, and interests. The companies then use this information, combined with information about the Web sites these customers visit, to target advertising at them—charging advertisers a premium for the ability to target their message to specific customers. NetZero, for example, keeps a small window open on its members' computer screens through which it directs a constant stream of targeted advertising at them. A NetZero customer who visits barnesandnoble.com, for example, is likely to see an ad for Amazon pop up in his window, while a user who visits ESPN.com may receive an ad for The Sports Authority, the sporting goods retailer.

While both of these business models are intuitively appealing, they are ultimately suspect. AOL's subscription revenues are nice because they provide a steady, annuity-like stream of income. Already, though, the growth of these revenues is slowing, as fewer new Internet users are coming on-line and those who do are turning to budget or free services. Though AOL executives flatly deny this, skeptics argue that at some point AOL's subscription revenues will decline as Internet users realize they're not getting a whole lot extra in exchange for their monthly fees. Though the spread of broadband may slow this erosion, a few companies are even experimenting with free broadband service, suggesting that subscription revenues as a source of income may diminish. Meanwhile, the fastest-growing part of AOL's business is advertising and commerce income—and ultimately, AOL's acquisition of Time Warner should bolster this side of its business.

At the same time, it's unclear whether an advertising-alone model such as NetZero's offers the perfect solution. While NetZero has had considerable success finding several million users willing to give away personal information and have their Web-surfing habits tracked in exchange for free Internet service, it faces intense competition in that area from portals and other Web sites offering the same kinds of free services. What's more, many Net users are nervous about companies tracking their movements across the Internet, suggesting that NetZero's ability to offer such highly targeted advertising may at some point be curtailed. That said, some form of advertising/commerce model is likely to win out; the question is simply whether it will be the type of targeted model advocated by NetZero or whether it will be a more basic, mass-market-type advertising model of the kind currently associated with television and radio.

The Softer Side of Infrastructure

Other firms traditionally considered part of the Internet infrastructure space are the software makers that design the programs that allow Web sites to run and that smooth the way for commerce and communications on-line. Unlike the other Internet infrastructure providers mentioned, these firms don't typically build machines, and they don't work with silicon or copper or fiber-optic cables. Instead, they're more akin to highly specialized brain trusts, where lots of smart people sit around programming computers. But the programs they create are critical, allowing other companies to quickly establish a presence on the Web or conduct transactions simply by purchasing off-the-shelf products. In the early days, for example, a Web retailer such as Amazon.com needed to have programmers on hand who could not just create the company's Web site from scratch but also design the behind-the-scenes infrastructure that allowed it to accept credit card payments or conduct instant searches by keyword. Now newcomers to the Web can simply buy those types of programs, ready-made, from software vendors. Included in this category are companies ranging from Microsoft to Oracle, which makes database software, to VeriSign and Entrust Technologies, which manufacture software and related technologies for secure Internet commerce and communications.

Company Snapshot: Oracle Corporation

At a Glance
Ticker symbol: ORCL
Founded: 1977
Went public: 1986
Fiscal 2000 revenue: $10.1 billion (year ended Sept. 30)
Revenue growth rate (vs. 1999): 14.8%
Fiscal 2000 profits: $2.1 billion (year ended Sept. 30)
Profit growth rate (vs. 1999): 61.5%
Key management: Larry Ellison, Chairman and CEO

Oracle's flagship product has been and remains its database software, which allows companies to manage vast quantities of information. Though it was around long before the advent of the commercial Internet, Oracle boasts that its software is now used by most of the largest Internet companies—and indeed it is, from Amazon.com to eBay to dozens of others. Amazon, for example, relies on Oracle software to store and serve up information on the thousands of products in its inventory.

Though database software is Oracle's mainstay, it is by no means its only product. The company is also a leader in the business-to-business world, where its products serve as the underlying architecture for some of the marketplaces used by companies to buy and sell goods and services. It is Oracle software, for example, that along with software developed by Commerce One serves as the backbone of the Covisint trade exchange developed by General Motors, Ford, and DaimlerChrysler. Oracle also develops a wide variety of other software used in managing corporations, from financial and human resources tools to customer relationship management software, used by companies to interact with clients and help track and answer their complaints or questions. Oracle has attempted to sell these various applications as a single software "suite," but it faces stiff competition from leaders within each category, such as Siebel Systems—a tenacious rival founded by an Oracle defector that now competes vigorously with Oracle to sell customer relationship management software.

Oracle doesn't just sell software; it also markets itself as a strategic adviser to its clients, consulting with them on how best to deploy and manage the software it sells them. Such consulting fees are becoming an important means for software companies of all stripes to develop recurring revenues as a supplement to their core licensing fees.

Obviously, different kinds of software have different market opportunities. Microsoft and Oracle, for example, which each started out making software that wasn't specifically aimed at the Internet, are now two of the largest companies in the world—and their founders are two of the world's wealthiest men. A brief word on each of these companies is in order. Microsoft's success came from creating the Windows operating system on which most personal computers run—a system so popular that the Justice Department succeeded in convincing a federal court to declare it a monopoly. Microsoft also created many of the programs that run on that underlying operating system—programs that have also become universally well known among consumers, including Microsoft Word for word processing, Microsoft Excel for creating spreadsheets, and Microsoft PowerPoint for putting together slide presentations.

Microsoft came late to the Internet and feared that its Windows operating system would ultimately be displaced by "browser" programs such as Netscape Navigator, which allow users to easily display Web sites and to surf from site to site. The company quickly devised a browser of its own, Internet Explorer, to compete with Navigator. And it was the decision to give Explorer away for free—and to bind it to every copy of Windows sold—that brought on the wrath of the Justice Department and the decision to sue Microsoft for abusing its monopoly.

With its business practices under assault and personal computer use expected to wane in coming years, Microsoft has found it a challenge to replicate its success on the desktop with its operating system for handheld devices such as cellular telephones and personal digital assistants. This software, Windows CE, faces competition from smaller companies, such as Palm, that have devised alternate systems of their own. Similarly, Microsoft has had somewhat less success on the corporate side, where its NT operating system is battling it out against the rival UNIX and Linux platforms, which many programmers prefer because they are easier to modify to their needs.

For its part, Oracle's success derives from its dominance of the database software market—a market that predates the Internet but has exploded in size and importance with the Net's rise. Though it isn't as well known among consumers, since they have little reason to use it, database software of the sort developed by Oracle is used to archive and sort huge volumes of information. As such, it's a linchpin of corporate computer networks and of the Internet. Consider Amazon.com, which not coincidentally happens to be an Oracle customer. Oracle's software is what allows Amazon to store photos and descriptions of the hundreds of thousands of products it offers for sale, as well as customer reviews of those products. So, too, for a huge percentage of the other leading e-commerce Web sites, as well as for other companies that need to archive and manipulate large quantities of information. What's more, Oracle's expertise in database technology has helped it become an eight-hundred-pound gorilla in a brand-new market that didn't exist just a few years ago—software to power the types of on-line trade exchanges discussed in Chapter Four.

Besides these two corporate giants, there are literally hundreds of different software companies producing thousands of different types of software applications ("application" is simply another word for a computer program). Few, if any, have as wide a potential target audience as Microsoft or Oracle. Still, there are a few with pretty huge potential markets. One of those is the encryption software that allows commerce and communications to be conducted securely over the Internet, with little fear of hackers' stealing it. VeriSign is the dominant player in this arena, but other players include companies such as Entrust Technologies, WatchGuard Technologies, Internet Security Systems, and Check Point Software Technologies. Another enormous category is software that allows audio and video material to be "streamed" over the Web. RealNetworks is the leader in this area, though it faces stiff competition from its Seattle neighbor Microsoft. A third big category is software that allows companies to build and maintain Web sites and to monitor Web site traffic, customer behavior, and on-line advertising effectiveness. A number of companies compete in this space, including Vignette and WebTrends.

While each of these companies has very different market opportunities and different business models, what they have in common is that the software business offers the potential for sizable profits. Creating software doesn't require heavy machinery or lots of raw materials; it requires only talented programmers. And once that software is created, reproducing it in quantity requires minimal additional effort and costs practically nothing. That, as you may recall, is the very definition of scalability. What's more, once the up-front investment is made, every additional sale represents incrementally more profit. That, of course, is the definition of leverage. While gross profit margins differ from firm to firm, of course, software makers typically have margins of 70 percent, and frequently as high as 80 percent and even 90 percent.

Beyond simply selling packages of software and occasional upgrades to that software—which can result in the kinds of "lumpy" and unpredictable earnings reports investors hate—many companies are coming up with new ways of deriving more reliable, annuity-like revenue streams from the software business. These companies, which have adopted the moniker "applications service providers," or ASPs, attempt to sell consulting services along with their software, with consultants available to help clients integrate complex programs into their businesses, train employees, and deal with problems as they arise. Many ASPs also "rent" software to their corporate clients for use on an as-needed basis, rather than selling it to them outright. For a client, renting avoids the need to shell out a large quantity of cash all at once to buy software that is ultimately likely to become outdated, or at least to require expensive upgrades. For a software company, renting is a way of keeping greater control over its product while ensuring a steady stream of revenues over time.

Company Snapshot: VeriSign

At a Glance
Ticker symbol: VRSN
Founded: 1995
Went public: 1998
2000 revenue: $474.8 million
Revenue growth rate (vs. 1999): 460%
2000 profits: $129.1 million
Profit growth rate (vs. 1999): 3128%
Key management: Stratton Sclavos, President and CEO

VeriSign is a software company whose products allow for the conduct of secure commerce across the Internet. Specifically, those products are so-called digital certificates—files encrypted with special codes that computers use to identify one another and exchange information privately. The certificates are used by a large number of companies and Web sites, ensuring that credit card numbers and communications are encrypted and locking out would-be snoops and cybercriminals. VeriSign is the leader in the digital certificate business, and many Web sites now proudly flaunt the VeriSign seal as an indicator to potential customers that they are safe places to do business. In addition, many companies use VeriSign's technology for internal communications and transactions.

In 1999, VeriSign purchased Network Solutions, the leading registrar of Internet domain names and the government-appointed keeper of the Internet domain-name registry. With the purchase, VeriSign acquired not just a steady stream of recurring revenues—in the form of the annual fee that accompanies every domain-name registration—but it also gained an enhanced opportunity to offer its other software and services to all the domain-name registrants that suddenly became its clients.

Anyhow, Anytime, Anywhere

It's been said of the Internet that, simple and convenient as it is to use, it isn't simple and convenient enough. What's meant by that, of course, is that the Net is frequently slow and not always reliable. Especially on dial-up connections, Web sites take time to download, and often they freeze up or crash. Until these glitches are overcome, it's said, the Web—for all its usefulness and popularity—won't truly become ubiquitous, an integral part of the lives of *most* ordinary people.

Another one of the Net's weaknesses is that it isn't portable. Right now, if you want to surf the Web—to trade a stock, say, or buy something from Amazon—you pretty much need to have a computer plugged into a phone line or a broadband connection. You could have a portable computer, of course—a laptop that you carry with you and can plug into any phone line, anywhere. But you still need to plug in to get on-line, and you pretty much need to stop whatever it is you're doing and sit still in order to do it.

Imagine how much more useful the Net would be if you didn't have to be sitting at your computer to access it, if you didn't need to stop what you were doing, or even sit still, to go on-line. Imagine, for example, that instead of accessing a Web site such as MapQuest.com—which will give you directions between practically any two locations—before you leave home, you could access it *while you're on the road* (or after you've gotten yourself lost). Or imagine that, while wandering around a new city, you suddenly have a craving for Vietnamese food, but you don't know where the nearest Vietnamese restaurant is. If only you had access to the Net—to a site such as Citysearch, for example, with its thousands of city-specific restaurant listings—you could find it. The good news is that that time is at hand—and it's going to make the Web that much bigger, more popular, and more useful than it already is.

Ever since its earliest days, network computing has had wireless access as one of its principal goals. And while there were some early efforts at getting computers to talk to one another via radio waves, only very recently has the effort truly gained momentum in a way that promises to Webify the wireless world. Soon, every cellular phone and every handheld personal digital assistant (along with more than a few wristwatches, in all likelihood) will be capable of accessing the Internet. As Internet analyst Michael Parekh of Goldman Sachs points out, "Mobile phones have all the necessary components needed to use the Internet—potential connectivity to the Internet through a wireless network, significant silicon content already on the phone, a display, and a power supply. As a result, Web-enabling the phone is a relatively straightforward task." What's more, he adds, "Web access from a mobile phone allows people to be connected anytime from just about anywhere . . . [and creates] the opportunity to make Internet users out of a large number of people that would otherwise not have the ability." Think about what this means in terms of Web usage. Already, far more people around the world have cell phones than have personal computers. By 2003, according to Goldman, the gap will be staggering: 1 billion cellular phone users, compared with half that many PC users. That's particularly significant in many Second and Third World countries, where computers and land-based telephones remain a rarity but cellular phones are spreading like wildfire (because they're relatively inexpensive and don't require a large installed infrastructure). Clearly, that bodes well for the Net and for companies doing business on-line, because it means more customers using the Web more frequently throughout their days. It also bodes well for the companies that make those devices—companies such as Motorola, Ericsson, and Nokia in the cell phone world, or Palm and Handspring in the PDA world—because it gives their products another reason to exist and their income statements another potential revenue stream. It also gives their customers another reason to be loyal. After all, if you've loaded all your Web bookmarks and personal information into your AT&T wireless phone, chances are you won't want to deal with the hassle of switching all that to a Sprint phone next time a slightly lower long-distance rate rolls around. This isn't an insignificant consideration. According to Goldman, between a quarter and a third of wireless phone customers switch operators every year. "By provisioning Internet services," Parekh suggests, "carriers can increase revenues through increased network utilization and e-commerce, lower costs through online customer care . . . and reduce churn through differentiation and personalization of [Internet] service offerings."

Besides the hardware makers, a whole new breed of companies has sprung up whose purpose is to make wireless devices such as phones and PDAs Internet-friendly: in Wall Street–speak, to "enable" them for the Net. The two biggest players in this space: Openwave Systems and InfoSpace. Both companies either reformat existing Internet content or create and assemble their own Web content for the small screens found on cellular phones and PDAs. While Openwave concentrates on providing the underlying software necessary to Web-enable wireless phones and PDAs, InfoSpace is focused more heavily on providing the information and commerce services that "lie on top" of those already Web-enabled devices. Thus, while the two companies compete in some ways, they are also occasional partners, and each can benefit, to some extent, from the other's success.

Interestingly, neither is seeking to push products under its own brand name. Rather, each allows customers—such as AT&T, Verizon, and Palm—to resell its services under their brand names. Customers of AT&T, for example, think they're using AT&T's Web portal when they log on to the Web from their cellular phones—although, in fact, they're using a portal designed by InfoSpace. That "private label" strategy accomplishes three things. It increases customers' loyalty to the carriers, it allows InfoSpace and Openwave to profit from increasing usage of the wireless Web, no matter which cell phone or PDA maker wins, and it reduces the marketing investments InfoSpace and Openwave themselves must make in branding their own services. As a result, the two companies operate highly efficient and potentially highly profitable business models. In general, InfoSpace and Openwave have several potential ways of generating revenue: they make money by licensing their software and services to their clients, they make a few dollars—under some contracts—every time one of those client's customers uses their services, and—depending on how the contracts are structured—they may make a few more dollars if those customers spend a lot of time using the Web. It's not hard to see how a few dollars per customer can add up quickly when we're talking about more than a billion potential customers. Additional profits may come from taking a slice of advertising or commerce transactions that are conducted over those wireless devices. For example, if my AT&T cell phone directs me, thanks to InfoSpace, to the nearest Burger King, InfoSpace and AT&T may share an advertising fee from Burger King, or even perhaps a tiny percentage of whatever business I do there. What's more, if I ask to be directed to Burger King, my cell phone might throw at me, in addition to those directions, a coupon for 10 percent off at the nearest McDonald's—another potential source of revenue for both InfoSpace and AT&T.

Finally, because the business is essentially a software business, it is both profit-heavy and—here come those buzzwords again—leveragable and scalable. Openwave's gross profit margins hover in the high 60 percent to low 70 percent range, and InfoSpace's in the low 80 percent range. Reformatting existing software for different clients' needs costs practically nothing, and once the cost of software development is recovered, each incremental sale or licensing fee falls almost directly to the companies' bottom line.

Company Snapshot: InfoSpace

At a Glance
Ticker symbol: INSP
Founded: 1996
Went public: 1998
2000 revenue: $214.6 million
Revenue growth rate (vs. 1999): 197%
2000 profits: $46.2 million
Profit growth rate (vs. 1999): NA
Key management: Naveen Jain, Chairman and CEO

Known throughout the Internet industry for his sharp tongue and outlandish predictions, InfoSpace founder Naveen Jain is only half kidding when he says InfoSpace aims to control 100 percent of the markets in which it does business and one day to become the first company with a $1 trillion market capitalization. "Monopolies aren't bad," says the Microsoft veteran, whose Seattle-area office—painted in bright primary colors that he himself selected—is only a short drive from his old employer. "It's abusing monopolies that's bad." But despite Jain's bold talk, InfoSpace remains a long way from 100 percent market share or a $1 trillion market cap.

Conceived as a company that would amass information and distribute it for other companies to use under their own brand names, InfoSpace's first offering was an on-line yellow pages, which it sold to portal sites operated by everyone from Microsoft to AOL. The company has extended this no-name strategy across a variety of offerings, allowing it to do business with a host of companies that are one anothers' fiercest competitors. InfoSpace is now focused most intently on the wireless arena, for which it creates software that allows cell phones to access the Internet. True to form, its customers include some of the biggest names—and most ardent rivals—in the wireless arena, from AT&T to VoiceStream to Verizon. Each of those companies uses InfoSpace software to offer everything from stock quotes to e-mail to comparison shopping services over their cell phones, under their own brand names. In 2000, InfoSpace acquired Go2Net, backed by Microsoft cofounder Paul Allen's Vulcan Ventures, in a bid to supplement its own offerings with Go2Net's medley of video games, community sites, and its own shopping software, as well as to aim more of its content at the growing broadband arena.

Making Sense of the Numbers

OK, so much for what Internet infrastructure companies do and how they do it. I promised we'd also talk about a few key performance measures you need to consider before picking a high-quality Internet infrastructure stock. Naturally, you want to start by looking at the same basic numbers you'd look for in any company, whether that company is in the business-to-consumer space, the business-to-business space, the infrastructure space, or outer space, for that matter. Those numbers are: the top line (revenue), the bottom line (profit) and the profit margin (the ratio of the bottom line to the top line). The bigger those numbers are and the faster they're growing from quarter to quarter and from year to year, the better shape the company is in. If they're not growing—or worse, if they're declining—it's probably best to stay away.

What's nice about Internet infrastructure companies, though, is that they tend to offer a high degree of what the analysts like to call "visibility." In other words, you can often get a pretty good idea of what's going to happen over the next several quarters from what happened this quarter. One reason for that is that companies tend not to just decide on the spur of the moment to buy customized big-ticket items such as routers or servers. They go through a long, complicated ordering process that generally results in the product's manufacture and delivery some considerable time after it was ordered. As a result, one way infrastructure companies have of giving Wall Street a hint about how well they're doing is their order backlog. The bigger that is, the more business they have lined up that hasn't actually shown up on the bottom line yet.

One way of measuring a company's order backlog is its *book-to-bill ratio*, usually disclosed in its quarterly earnings report. This clunky term simply refers to the ratio of new orders received—and therefore *booked*—versus orders already shipped—and therefore *billed* and incorporated into the existing sales numbers. A book-to-bill ratio of 1 means the company has as many orders left to fill as it has just filled (in other words, its business is steady). A book-to-bill ratio of less than 1 means business is slowing down, and a book-to-bill ratio of greater than 1 means business is picking up. So what do you want to look for? You guessed it: a book-to-bill ratio of greater than one. The greater, the better.

Even once orders are billed, though, they aren't necessarily paid for right away, so another important measure of a company's financial health is how quickly it's able to collect payments from its customers. Fortunately, Wall Street's accounting wizards have devised a single numerical indicator that describes exactly that: "day-sales outstanding," which measures the number of days it takes to collect payment on a dollar's worth of sales. While this isn't a hard number to calculate (it's just accounts receivable—money owed but not yet paid—divided by total sales for that quarter, times 91, which is the average number of days in a quarter), most companies make it easy by doing the math for us. And while there's no single benchmark of how many DSOs are considered acceptable, the lower the number, the better. Even more important is that the number either stays stable or falls, and that it not trend higher over time. An increasing level of DSOs would suggest that a company is having a harder time getting its clients to pay their bills—or, worse, that it's stuffing its pipeline with goods clients don't want in an effort to artificially inflate its sales numbers.

One last number deserves some attention: inventory turns, which measures the speed with which a company is able to move goods out of its warehouse—or, alternately, the amount of time it's sitting on that inventory, waiting for it to be sold. Again, it isn't hard to do the math here (divide total sales by average inventory), but most companies break this number out in their quarterly earnings reports. Here you're looking for a relatively high number or one that's increasing. The reason? A company that sits on inventory for a long time is losing money in two ways: it has to pay for the storage of that inventory, and it isn't earning any money from it. Beyond that, low inventory turnover is a sign of inefficiency and inability to gauge customer needs, while high inventory turnover indicates just the opposite. What's more, chances are that a company that turns its inventory frequently is one whose products are in high demand. And that's perhaps the ultimate indicator of a company's chances of success.

CHAPTER SIX

Sneaking in the Back Door

Internet Investing by Proxy

AT LAST, the chapter for those of you who—notwithstanding everything you've read so far—still don't have the stomach for pure-play dot-com stocks. Yes, you want to invest in the Internet. No, you don't want to miss out on the economic revolution that's under way. But you also want to sleep at night, and you're just not quite convinced you're going to be able to pick the long-term winners from the fly-by-nights. We've already discussed a handful of ways you, too, can participate in the Internet boom: putting your money to work behind bricks-and-mortar retailers such as Wal-Mart and Kmart, for example, that are making serious forays into on-line commerce, or companies such as Cisco and Sun that are building the Internet's physical backbone. But there's another way you can dip your toe into the water. It's called "proxy investing." And it's essentially a way of sneaking in the back door of the Internet while still being able to look your friends squarely in the eye and tell them you're a buttoned-down, conservative shareholder in some of the bluest of this nation's blue-chip companies. For you, the story of Levi Strauss is worth remembering.

Strauss, you may recall, made his fortune during the California gold rush of the nineteenth century, when thousands of prospectors trekked out west to pan for the precious metal. Like the most aggressive of today's dot-com speculators—who hope they'll be among the lucky few to pick a big winner while it's still in its infancy—the '49ers, as they became known, hoped to strike it rich by rummaging through tons of worthless dirt and finding gold. Strauss figured theirs was a long-shot venture, at best. Rather than join them, he realized that all those gold miners were going to need tents and work clothes. That realization prompted him to start selling his now-famous pants made of denim and held together with metal studs—racking up enormous profits even as precious few of his customers ended up finding anything precious at all. So, too, for other entrepreneurs who made small fortunes selling the less fortunate miners the picks and shovels they needed to do their jobs.

More recently, billionaire investor Walter Annenberg made his megafortune in a similar way at the birth of another revolutionary new communications medium: television. Hundreds of TV-set-manufacturing companies sprang up and then fell by the wayside. RCA was one example of a company that saw its stock soar on the assumption that it would dominate the TV manufacturing industry. Instead, it was overtaken by more efficient Japanese rivals—which leapfrogged ahead with cheaper, better-made models—and its stock ultimately plunged. (Ironically, that was the second time this sort of thing had happened to RCA. In the 1920s, investors scrambled to buy its shares, along with those of a slew of other companies, amid the boom in radio production. RCA—the Radio Corporation of America—-saw its stock zoom 100-fold before the Crash of 1929, when it was decimated. Most of its formerly high-flying competitors went out of business. But RCA survived—its stock recovered its 1920s highs amid the 1950s TV boom—only to fall by the wayside once again and ultimately be acquired by General Electric.) Other companies of the early TV age, meanwhile, hoped to profit by creating and distributing content for the fledgling new medium. These television networks—ABC, CBS, and NBC—were successful, though in later decades they, too, lost luster as competitors sprang up and as the introduction of cable TV fragmented their audience. In the long run, none was able to survive as an independent company. Annenberg, meanwhile, took a different route. Rather than invest in TV itself—or in the creation and distribution of content—he put his money to work backing a small magazine that offered listings of everything that was playing on the various networks. That publication, *TV Guide*, became the indispensable tool that millions of Americans had to have to know what was on—whether they ended up watching ABC, NBC or CBS, whether their sets were made by RCA, Sony, or Magnavox. And so it was that television helped make Walter Annenberg a billionaire, even though he never manufactured a single TV set or created a single TV program.

Company Snapshot: Motorola

At a Glance
Ticker symbol: MOT
Founded: 1920
Went public: 1943
2000 revenue: $37.6 billion
Revenue growth rate (vs. 1999): 17%
2000 profits: $1.9 billion
Profit growth rate (vs. 1999): 36%
Key management: Christopher Galvin, Chairman and CEO

Motorola became a leader in the cellular phone business early on, having manufactured the first clunky versions of the phones that were used by the U.S. military to communicate with troops in the thick of battle. After adapting the cell phones to consumer use, Motorola then lagged in updating the products, particularly as more and more customers progressed from the early analog versions to more advanced digital phones that offered better sound quality. Almost overnight, the company lost its market lead to a pair of Nordic rivals—Nokia of Finland and Ericsson of Sweden—that won consumers over with smaller, more eye-catching designs.

More recently, however, Motorola has roared back into the cell phone space with a renewed commitment to creating more fashionable cell phones, reclaiming some of the market share it had previously lost. The company is now well positioned to benefit from an ongoing explosion in the wireless market, not just in the United States and Europe—where cell phones have become ubiquitous, used for accessing the Internet as well as carrying on traditional conversations—but also in Second and Third World nations. There, cellular phone systems are popping up in places where an infrastructure for traditional wired phones never existed.

But Motorola is far from just a cellular phone maker. Among other things, the company is a major player in the semiconductor industry, manufacturing chips that are used both in its own cellular devices and in the set-top boxes used to receive cable television signals. Thus, while its fortunes tend to rise and fall with those of the ever-cyclical semiconductor business, Motorola stands to prosper as more and more consumers begin to use their television sets and cable lines—not to mention their cellular phones—to surf the Web.

Get the idea? Both Strauss and Annenberg made their money not by investing *directly* in the boom that was happening around them but by investing *indirectly*—on the periphery—in businesses that would benefit from the sheer fact that the boom was happening. When it came down to it, it didn't matter much to Strauss whether anybody made money by striking gold—as long as enough people believed that they might and so journeyed west to give it their best shot (buying his tents and work clothes along the way). Nor did Annenberg really care who built the most TV sets or created and distributed the most TV content—as long as people were watching. Both men stood to profit no matter who emerged the winner. This is what's known as "proxy investing," because the investment serves in place of (or as a proxy for) a direct bet on the underlying phenomenon. I like to think of it as backdoor investing, because you're essentially sneaking into the trend through a back door.

The Internet is chock full of backdoor investment opportunities. There are obvious ones, such as Dell, Compaq, Apple Computer, and Gateway, which make the computers people use to go on-line, as well as Intel and Advanced Micro Devices, which make the chips that power the computers that people use to go on-line. These companies existed before the age of the Internet, and their products serve functions other than Web surfing, but they are benefiting from the Internet's growing popularity. Other backdoor investments are a little less obvious, which naturally makes them a lot more interesting. Consider: everybody who goes on-line needs an Internet connection, provided by one of the Internet service providers discussed in Chapter Five. But that Internet service provider is shipping that data traffic around on cables leased from companies such as AT&T, WorldCom, and Qwest. These aren't Internet companies, per se. But the explosion in data being sent back and forth and around the Web means an explosion in traffic on their networks—and hence a profit opportunity for them. And what about all the companies that pack and ship the goods consumers order from Internet retailers—such as Fingerhut (a unit of Federated Department Stores), FedEx (a unit of FDX Corporation), and UPS? As more things are ordered via the Web, they stand to benefit as well. This indirect investment strategy can be taken out to several degrees of separation from pure-play dot-com investing. There are the Wall Street investment banks—such as Goldman Sachs, Morgan Stanley, and Merrill Lynch—that underwrite Internet-related stock offerings and advise on mergers among Internet companies. There are the real estate firms—particularly those with office space in Silicon Valley or New York City—that rent their properties to dot-com companies. There are the advertising agencies, TV networks, and billboard companies that are the recipients of dot-com advertising largesse. Some of these minibooms will fade as quickly as they arose. Some already have, as the Internet IPO boom has subsided and the Internet advertising glut has ebbed. But others—like the surge in data traffic on telecommunications networks or the increase in packages shipped from on-line retailers—are likely to be more permanent, creating longer-term investment opportunities. A few of these are worth examining in closer detail.

Company Snapshot: Gateway

At a Glance
Ticker symbol: GTW
Founded: 1985
Went public: 1993
2000 revenue: $9.7 billion
Revenue growth rate (vs. 1999): 7.7%
2000 profits: $448 million
Profit growth rate (vs. 1999): 3%
Key management: Theodore Waitt, Chairman
and CEO

Gateway is a prime example of a personal computer company that is using the Internet to its fullest advantage—as a sales and customer service channel for its core products, as well as a source of additional revenues as a product in and of itself. The company has three primary channels through which it sells its product: the telephone (customers can place orders over Gateway's toll-free number), the Internet (customers can place orders directly over the Net), and the company's own Gateway Country stores, located in major cities across the country. The phone and Internet services allow Gateway to maintain contact directly with its customers at relatively low cost, avoiding middlemen. The Country stores, while a more expensive channel to operate, offer consumers who need it a chance to "touch and feel" Gateway's products before buying. Those consumers can later be converted onto the telephone and Internet channels.

Gateway derives the bulk of its revenues from selling and leasing desktop computers. But the company has also teamed with AOL to operate its Gateway.net Internet access service, which it bundles together with many of the computers it sells. In this way, while it has handed off the operation of the Internet service to a recognized leader in that area, Gateway nonetheless manages to derive a noteworthy and growing percentage of its business—nearly a quarter of its revenues as of year end 2000—by supplementing its core product with an additional offering many of its customers desire, thereby keeping for itself revenues that would otherwise likely go to a third party. Gateway and AOL are also teaming to develop stripped-down Internet "appliances" for users who wish to access the Net but don't need or want to pay for a full-service computer.

Company Snapshot: Palm

At a Glance
Ticker symbol: PALM
Founded: 1996
Went public: 2000
Fiscal 2001 revenue: $923.2 million (through fiscal Q2)
Revenue growth rate (vs. 2000): 112%
Fiscal 2001 profits: $51.4 million (through fiscal Q2)
Profit growth rate (vs. 2000): 102%
Key management: Carl Yankowski, CEO

Originally a unit of U.S. Robotics and later of 3Com (which acquired U.S. Robotics in 1997), Palm was spun out as a separately traded entity in 2000. Its name has become synonymous with the handheld computers known as personal digital assistants, or PDAs, that have themselves become an icon of the Internet age. Palm's signature product, the PalmPilot, is essentially a personal organizer, with an address book, calendar, memo pad, and even a few video games built in. As successive generations of the Pilot have become smaller, sleeker, and faster, it has also gained expanded memory and functionality, including the ability to access the Internet and surf the Web via a wireless modem, and even to serve as a cellular phone.

But if it was the first and best-known maker of PDAs, Palm is by no means without competition from rivals like Compaq, Sony, and upstart Handspring, a company founded by the two executives who founded Palm itself. What's more, at some point the convergence of PDAs with other handheld devices portends additional competitors in Palm's space. Ultimately, after all, it seems unlikely that consumers will want to carry around a separate pager, cellular phone, and MP3 player to play back music downloaded from the Internet. That convergence could pit Palm against such giants as Motorola and Nokia, as well as smaller players like Research In Motion, maker of the BlackBerry wireless e-mail device. What's more, while its operating system for the PalmPilot is currently the standard—providing a source of additional licensing revenues from rivals such as Handspring—Palm faces deep-pocketed rivals in that space as well, including Microsoft, which is pushing its own Windows CE operating system for handheld computers.

It's the Computer, Stupid!

Sometimes things are so blatantly obvious that we tend to overlook them. Here's one: everybody who wants to go on-line needs a device to get on-line. Chances are it'll be a computer. But increasingly, it doesn't have to be. It could be a personal digital assistant, such as a PalmPilot. Or it could be a cellular phone. What's more, every single one of those Internet access devices is powered by a little silicon wafer known as a microchip. The pros of the computer and Internet appliance business are that it is fast growing and composed of a relatively limited number of leading players within each subsector. The top makers of desktop and laptop computers, for example, are Dell, Compaq, Apple, and Gateway. The dominant makers of personal digital assistants are Palm and Handspring. The giants of the cellular phone handset industry are Motorola and Nokia. Within the chip space, leaders are Intel and AMD for computer chips, Broadcom, Applied Micro Circuits, and PMC-Sierra for various types of communication chips, and Applied Materials among chip equipment makers (companies that make the machines that chip makers need to make chips).

The cons are that, notwithstanding the rapid growth and relatively small number of top contestants, these companies are not immune to their share of blowups: witness recent disasters at Apple, Compaq, and Motorola. Price wars are frequent, and technology competition is brutal. In fact, the biggest threat to companies in this Net appliance sector is probably the speed of the sector's growth—and the fact that the products people use to access the Web are likely to look very different in a few years than they look today. And while the same threat faces all technology companies, it seems particularly true here. Ultimately, for example, Web surfers won't divide their time between a primary desktop or laptop computer at home or at the office, a PDA they carry around, and a cellular phone, all of which not only offer Internet and e-mail access but also store various versions of schedules, to-do lists, and address books. More likely is that at least some of these devices will converge. And while it's possible that Dell, Compaq, Apple, Gateway, Palm, Microsoft, Motorola, and Nokia (not to mention IBM, Hewlett-Packard, Sony, and others) will all emerge unscathed from this technology product cycle, it's probable that at least some of these companies will stumble along the way—or be displaced by their rivals' superior technology.

Which leads to an obvious question: how to avoid the stumbles? The bad news is that unless you're a soothsayer, it isn't easy. The good news is that, as consumer products companies, it's not terribly hard to tell which of these Net appliance makers is winning the hearts, minds, and dollars of consumers at any given time. Just look around and see what devices people are using. That'll give you some sense not just of whose products are proving popular but also of who's innovating in a way that's likely to keep them at the forefront of technological change and consumers' tastes. There are also more scientific ways of doing the same thing: check out not just a company's revenue growth (is it speeding up or slowing down?) but also its research and development budget (is it growing or shrinking?). R-and-D spending may not be a perfect measure, but it's at least a decent indicator of how much innovation is likely down the road.

Company Snapshot: Intel

At a Glance
Ticker symbol: INTC
Founded: 1968
Went public: 1971
2000 revenue: $33.7 billion
Revenue growth rate (vs. 1999): 15%
2000 profits: $12.1 billion
Profit growth rate (vs. 1999): 49%
Key management: Andy Grove, Chairman; Craig Barrett, CEO

The phrase "Intel Inside" has become a hallmark of the personal computer era, and, as it suggests, Intel is by far the dominant maker of the microchips that power desktop computers. Indeed, the company's growth over the decade of the 1990s and into the early part of the 2000s was nothing short of phenomenal.

That said, Intel does face competition, including an intense rivalry with the far smaller Advanced Micro Devices that leads to periodic price wars. Though AMD's technology has generally been considered somewhat inferior to Intel's, it recently introduced a chip that, for the first time, was faster than Intel's premium product—putting Intel in the unaccustomed position of playing catch-up. A far newer arrival on the chip-making scene is upstart Transmeta, whose Crusoe chip promises performance comparable to that of Intel's products at far lower energy levels. Transmeta has won contracts to provide chips for laptop computers to clients ranging from Sony to Fujitsu to NEC. Though Intel shows few signs yet of losing significant market share, the rapid rise of Transmeta and the recent success of AMD suggest that Intel's future dominance is by no means assured if the company cannot stay at the forefront of new technologies.

What's more, concerned by the potential long-term decline of the desktop computer business, Intel has lately begun to experiment with developing other consumer electronic products. Though none of these has yet moved far beyond the conceptual stage, the idea is to extend Intel's well-recognized and well-regarded brand name into other areas. But that strategy of branching out into untested waters is not without risk—including the prospect of losing focus on its core competency at a time when competition in that business is intensifying.

Reach Out and E-Mail Someone

Anyone who was awake for even a small part of the 1990s has no doubt heard the phrase "Information Superhighway." Hackneyed as it now is, the expression actually conjures up a pretty accurate mental picture of how the Internet works. In Chapter Five, I looked at the Net's physical infrastructure: the server and storage computers, and the switches and routers, that store, steer, and translate the reams of data that are what we think of when we think of the Internet. What I alluded to but didn't talk about are the paths these bits and bytes of information travel when they're not being stored or translated. These paths, it turns out, are nothing more than copper or fiber-optic cables, more or less like the ones that have been used by telephone companies to carry our phone conversations for years. Now they're carrying Internet data. While there are some firms, such as Qwest, Global Crossing, and Genuity, that are focused largely on deploying and operating these kinds of pipes to carry data traffic, many of them are operated by the same companies that operate regular phone lines.

The Internet, as it turns out, couldn't have come along at a better time for companies such as Ma Bell—just as their core long-distance business was fading into unprofitability. It's not that long-distance calling has suddenly become unpopular. Quite the contrary. After two decades of escalating competition from upstart rivals such as WorldCom, Sprint, and more recently, local phone companies, long-distance calling has become a commodity, with rates falling precipitously. A phone call from New York to Los Angeles that AT&T used to be able to charge, say, 25 cents a minute for now fetches a nickel or less per minute. That is money that has come straight out of Ma Bell's bottom line. And that rapid plunge in profits has caused all sorts of chaos in the long-distance business.

Along came the Internet, and with it an explosion in the demand for "pipes" to carry data traffic. Ever since AOL's revolutionary decision in 1997 to charge one flat rate for unlimited monthly usage, time spent on-line has soared, even as the cost to the consumer of going on-line has plunged. But here's the rub: even though all those minutes on-line don't cost you, the consumer, anything, they do cost your Internet service provider money. Whether your provider is AOL or NetZero, it no doubt has an agreement with a telecommunications provider such as AT&T or WorldCom to carry all that data traffic. Generally, an ISP buys huge blocks of time from the telecom company at discounted rates. For the ISP, this results in a Catch-22: it wants you to spend time on-line so it can throw advertising at you, but every minute you spend on-line is costing it money. But for the telecom company, it's a huge boon.

All this said, it's worth remembering that an investment in the phone company isn't likely to make you rich. There's a reason Ma Bell was, for years, known as a "widows-and-orphans" stock. It's widely held, and—until its late-2000 restructuring—it paid a nice dividend. But it was never a barn burner. At the same time, newer, faster-growing entrants to the sector, such as Global Crossing and Qwest, may prove more appealing for somewhat more aggressive investors.

Company Snapshot: WorldCom

At a Glance
Ticker symbol: WCOM
Founded: 1983
Went public: 1989
2000 revenue: $39.1 billion
Revenue growth rate (vs. 1999): 8.9%
2000 profits: $4.7 billion
Profit growth rate (vs. 1999): 18.8%
Key management: Bernard Ebbers, Chairman and CEO

Along with AT&T, one of the largest of the nation's long-distance providers, WorldCom has been transformed by the explosion in data traffic over the Internet and the simultaneous

precipitous decline in its long-distance business, where revenues have dropped along with rates. Though the decline in long distance was long foretold as more and more players got into the business and per minute rates for phone calls plunged, the speed of its demise came as a surprise to both WorldCom and AT&T. Ultimately, it led to radical restructurings at both companies, with AT&T splitting itself into four component companies over several years and WorldCom issuing a tracking stock for its consumer business—MCI—while maintaining the business services and data business under its own name.

The product of a steady stream of ever-larger acquisitions, WorldCom's purchase of a company called UUNET in 1996 instantly catapulted it into a leading position in the Internet backbone business, where it stands to benefit from the exponential increase in data traffic over the Web. The risk is that data transport is ultimately a commodity business, so that—as with the long-distance voice business—WorldCom's profitability depends on demand rising more quickly than supply. In 2000, WorldCom struck a deal to acquire control of Digex, one of the larger Web-hosting companies, making the company a leading player in that business as well, able to package its data transport and hosting services in a bid to compete with Web-hosting giants such as Exodus Communications. Notwithstanding these deals, which have positioned the company to grow along with the Internet, WorldCom remains, for the moment, a telephone company at its core, with its future still heavily dependent on the fortunes of that business.

The Heavy Lifting

Did you ever wonder what happens *after* you place an order at an Internet retailer? Who does all the heavy lifting of getting that book from Amazon.com in Seattle or buy.com in Mission Viejo, California, to your doorstep in just a couple of days? Turns out, the answer isn't the same for both companies.

The process of getting an item from an Internet retailer to you is called "distribution" or "fulfillment." Some companies, such as

Amazon.com and Webvan, handle their own fulfillment. These companies have spent millions, even billions, of dollars building giant distribution centers of hundreds of thousands of square feet each in cities across the country. Even though building and operating these centers is costly and labor-intensive, these companies view handling their own fulfillment as a competitive advantage. They believe they can provide better customer service if they handle every step in the distribution process, maintain their own inventory, and never let go of their customer lists. In fact, both companies have gotten so good at fulfillment—Webvan guarantees that its orders will reach customers within a specified one-hour window—that they hope to charge other companies for fulfilling orders on their behalf. Dominating the "last mile" of distribution is a fundamental part of Webvan's business model. The company aims to develop alliances with other Internet retailers to distribute their products for them. Amazon, meanwhile, has allied with Toys "R" Us to use Amazon's distribution capabilities to handle fulfillment for Toys "R" Us's Web site—now featured on Amazon.com—with the two companies sharing the proceeds. Amazon officials have even considered the possibility of one day spinning off the distribution centers as a separate, publicly traded entity.

Company Snapshot: United Parcel Service of America

At a Glance
Ticker symbol: UPS
Founded: 1907
Went public: 1999
2000 revenue: $29.8 billion
Revenue growth rate (vs. 1999): 10.1%
2000 profits: $2.8 billion
Profit growth rate (vs. 1999): 20.2%
Key management: James Kelly, Chairman and CEO

Hardly identified in most people's minds as a "new-economy company," UPS instead connotes drab brown trucks filled with cardboard boxes of all shapes and sizes. Ironically, though, this company—along with rivals such as FedEx and even the U.S. Postal Service—could benefit enormously from the advent of the Internet as a consumer tool. Collectively, these companies dominate the "last mile" between the Internet and the customer and play a vital role in fulfillment—the process of picking, packing, and delivering goods ordered via the Net.

Think about it: just about every product ordered from an on-line store—whether it be a book, a toaster, or a computer—needs to be moved from that store's distribution center to the customer's door. Most of the time, that means using the services of companies such as UPS, FedEx, and the Postal Service.

There's nothing terribly difficult to understand about UPS's business, other than that it is logistically extremely complex. It is also extremely capital-intensive, requiring fleets of trucks and airplanes as well as massive distribution centers and thousands of employees. As a result, while the profit margins are relatively low, the barriers to entry are quite high. That means that while demand for the company's services will keep rising, the risk of upstarts suddenly stealing the company's business is relatively remote.

Other companies, such as buy.com, handle none of their own distribution. These companies are entirely virtual—they operate only their Web sites and nothing more. In theory, this makes for very high profit margins, since these companies hold no inventory and operate no warehouses. But it also means they have to depend on third-party distributors to do everything for them once an order is placed, and that they have less direct control over how those orders are handled. (Buy.com is actually partly owned by the same people who own the closely held Ingram distribution companies, one of the nation's biggest fulfillment specialists, and uses Ingram to handle most of its fulfillment.) Not surprisingly, given this model, buy.com has generally ranked lower than Amazon in customer service surveys, though it has seen its ratings improve over time.

Just as there are companies that handle none of their own distribution, there are also companies that do nothing but handle distribution for others. There are several different types of third-party fulfillment specialists. Some, including Ingram and also the Fingerhut unit of Federated Department Stores, handle the entire back end of distribution, from stockpiling the inventory to packing and shipping an order once it's placed. Others handle the order from the moment it leaves the warehouse until the moment it arrives on your doorstep. These are organizations such as the U.S. Postal Service, FDX (parent of FedEx), and UPS. No matter which retailers emerge the winners in e-commerce, companies like UPS and FDX stand to benefit, as long as e-commerce itself becomes popular. Thus, they're worth considering as potential Internet-related investments, particularly for relatively conservative investors. An investment in UPS or FDX, after all, may fluctuate in value. But it's a fairly safe bet that your principal won't disappear entirely.

Security Comes at a Price

As you might suspect, though, just as they aren't likely to disappear overnight, these types of backdoor investments aren't likely to suddenly explode in value, either. For one thing, fulfillment companies aren't virtual businesses, so they don't offer the benefits of a virtual cost structure. Dot-com beneficiary or not, UPS is still what Wall Street denizens call "capital-intensive": it must operate an enormous and expensive fleet of trucks and airplanes and maintain thousands of drivers and pilots on its payroll in order to move packages from one place to another. As efficient as the company might be, the business itself is not terribly efficient. UPS's operating profits before taxes generally amount to about 15 percent of its revenues. That's actually not bad. FDX's profit margin is less than half that. Generally speaking, fulfillment companies feature relatively fat expense structures and thin profit margins. The argument in their favor is that they're likely to do more business and make more money, given all the things that are being ordered over the Net, than they did previously.

On the other hand, even in spite of the big boost it's getting from the boom in e-commerce, the fulfillment and distribution industry isn't exactly growing at barn-burning rates. Long-term, the air and ground shipping business is growing at only about 4 percent a year, according to Goldman Sachs. And it's very sensitive to economic cycles. During the recession of 1991, FDX saw its overnight shipping business decline 6 percent.

Fulfillment companies are also more sensitive to things such as rising interest rates and higher oil prices than their virtual counterparts. FDX, for example, carries more than $1 billion in debt on its books—necessary to finance all that infrastructure but costly as well, to the tune of $100 million a year or more in interest expense. FDX, UPS, and their rivals also spend between 2.5 and 4 percent of their revenues just on fuel to power all those trucks and fly all those planes. If fuel prices rise, their cost of doing business rises as well. Then, too, there are the mundane sort of worries—weather, labor issues—that such companies need to worry about that are much less of an issue in the virtual world. It's worth remembering that as recently as 1997, UPS was brought to its knees by a strike that crippled its financial performance that year.

One other risk is worth keeping in mind: virtual distribution. For some things, such as clothes, computers, or furniture, fulfillment companies will always be needed to move the product from a warehouse to your door. But for others, such as books, music, and software, the distribution intermediaries are already being displaced. Increasingly, those items are being distributed right over the Web. Already, various technologies allow books, software, and music to be downloaded directly to desktop computers or even to handheld devices such as PalmPilots and MP3 players. Devices like these make it that much easier to order products over the Web and have them delivered instantly—but it means they may be delivered in virtual, rather than physical, form. While such virtual media are still a small part of the market, their popularity is growing fast. And other products are starting to "go virtual" as well, from videos to airline tickets. For fulfillment specialists, it's an unfortunate coincidence that these are among the most popular items for consumers to order over the Web.

CHAPTER SEVEN

What's It Worth to Ya?

Valuation and
The Portfolio Approach

STOCK MARKET RISK is often defined as the likelihood that at any given moment the return on your investment isn't what you expected it to be. That risk is often expressed in terms of volatility, which is the frequency with which and extent to which a stock price fluctuates. The extreme volatility of the Internet sector overall and of the categories within that sector is one reason Internet investing has been deemed so risky. But it isn't the only reason. Internet investing has also earned its reputation for high-wire walking because investors have been willing to pay huge sums of money to own shares of companies that have never earned a profit and have little likelihood of earning one in the near future. That penchant for paying so much to obtain so little has called into question the entire concept of trying to assign a value to a stock based on its future earnings potential.

Those who have bought shares at what seem hugely inflated prices have argued that the "old-fashioned" methods of valuing stocks don't apply to the Internet, with its rapid growth and immense potential to alter the world. Skeptics counter that the players in that part of the stock market aren't investors but speculators. The evidence to date—the formation and collapse of several "bubbles" in Internet stock prices—indicates that the skeptics generally are right. As a group, Internet stock prices have fallen 40 percent or more from their highs at least five times between 1995 and 2000, according to data compiled by Merrill Lynch. That certainly indicates the presence of something more than sober-minded stock analysis at work in the pricing of Internet stocks. Further evidence that emotion—or at least something other than logic—is at work is the fickle nature of the most active Internet investors, or speculators. They flock to one subsector of the Internet, driving prices into the stratosphere, and then abandon it—causing a subsequent plunge in prices—to chase stocks in another subsector to death-defying heights. The prospect of being stuck with a bunch of overvalued Internet stocks in free fall is enough to scare away any investor who thinks there should be some logical reason to buy a stock.

For a good part of the mid- to late 1990s, it seemed as though anything with a dot com in its name, no matter what its business model or its prospects for success, was guaranteed an eye-popping initial public stock offering. The very first of these offerings was Netscape, which went public in early August 1995 at $28 a share and opened for trading at $71, giving it a market capitalization of more than $2 billion even though the company had never earned a dime. In its wake, other dot coms that were bleeding red ink decided they, too, could take advantage of the market's willingness to believe in the future of the Net and take the rest on faith. During this time, many stocks with little or no revenue and massive losses saw their stocks reach stratospheric levels in their first few days of trading, giving their companies values in the billions of dollars. This larger dot-com bubble was actually composed of a series of smaller bubbles: one for B2C stocks, one for B2B stocks, and one for infrastructure stocks, each of which had their day in the sun at a time when investors showed little enthusiasm for the others. A large number of investors who got caught up in the euphoria lost money, as most of these stocks spent the next few years losing ground.

The key lesson to take away from this series of bursting bubbles is that the stock market, however rational it might be over the long term, frequently suffers from a form of manic depression in the short term: either it loves a sector or it hates it. For long-term investors who pick stocks carefully and for good reasons and don't allow themselves to be swayed by momentary, stomach-turning gyrations, this can be good news. It means that every once in a while, high-quality companies that were previously very expensive go on sale. The lesson? If your horizon is years instead of months, you can afford to view these occasional dips as buying opportunities. The risk? Failing to recognize the "rational" sell-offs—the ones that actually are the result of some fundamental change in business conditions or in a particular company's profit potential. Trite as it sounds, you can't afford to grow complacent. More often than not, when "the market" sours on a particular group of stocks, it punishes the best of companies along with the worst of companies; stock market analysts refer to this, rather inelegantly, as "throwing out the baby with the bathwater." The best thing to do in these situations is to sit tight or even bulk up on those stocks that are being unfairly punished. On the other hand, every once in a while, the market is dead on. Your job as an investor is to try to distinguish the occasions when fundamentals actually have changed from the occasions when they haven't.

Methinks I've Seen This Before

One bit of good news is that market behavior and investor mentality are, to some extent, predictable in that they tend to follow patterns over time. Bank stocks, for example, tend to be weak when interest rates are rising, based in part on a traditional belief that rising rates shrink the spread between the interest banks charge on loans and the interest they pay out on deposits. As it turns out, this financial equation is less and less accurate as banks in recent years have diversified their revenues away from lending into recurring fee-for-service businesses such as money management. Nonetheless, bank stocks continue to be weak in rising rate environments. Similarly, retail stocks tend to be strong in the fourth quarter, as investors grow excited over the prospect of strong holiday sales, and weaker in the first quarter, as the holiday euphoria wears off (and people start to return unwanted gifts).

These types of cyclical and seasonal patterns are apparent even among the relatively young stocks that make up the Internet sector. What's more, they're often exaggerated because of the number of day traders and momentum-oriented investors who like to pile in when stocks are moving up or down and who have proven particularly partial to volatile Internet shares. Just as with ordinary retailers, consumer-oriented Internet companies tend to run up in the weeks and months leading up to Christmas and then sell off again in the weeks and months afterward. A couple of firms, notably eBay, the person-to-person auction site, and Priceline, which lets consumers bid on items ranging from airline tickets to rental cars, exhibit slightly different behavior. eBay tends to do somewhat less business in the weeks before Christmas (who, after all, wants to give away secondhand tchatchkes as a gift?) than it does in the weeks afterward (as thousands of gift recipients try to unload unwanted presents!). Priceline also does better after the holiday, when the airlines have a greater inventory of unsold seats they're trying to dispose of through alternate channels (of which Priceline is one). Generally speaking, Net stocks tend to be weak over the summer months, as investors and Internet users alike spend time outdoors, on the beach, and away from their computers, and strong again in the fall, as students return to school, the days grow shorter, and time spent on-line increases (along with time spent looking after one's investments, trying to recover the cost of that lavish summer vacation!). Each quarter, many Net stocks run up slightly in advance of their earnings reports, on the expectation of good news, and sell off afterwards, on the realization of that news or in the event of bad news.

These patterns are prime examples of how the market may be emotion-driven in the short term, reverting to more rational behavior over the long term. For the savvy investor, they represent excellent opportunities to establish positions, expand positions, or trim positions in particular stocks. If I know, for example, that shares of XYZ.com are likely to run up in December and fall back in January, I might want to take advantage of that December surge to take some profits and reduce my exposure to the stock, or I might want to use that January sell-off to build my stake. On the other hand, it's probably not a good idea to depend on such patterns too much. If some fundamental change clouds the long-term business prospects of a company in which you have a big stake, for example, you may want to get out of that position sooner, rather than wait for the possibility of a Christmastime run-up and possibly end up disappointed.

How Much Is That Dot Com in the Window?

Now we come to the key question: How does one figure out how much an Internet company is worth? Valuation, as this process is called, is at once the easiest, the most difficult, and the most important aspect of any investment, not just Internet stocks. It's the easiest because in the long run, a company's market value should always correspond directly to its expected future profits, discounted for the time it will take to achieve those profits, the risk that they won't ever materialize, and what else that invested money could be doing in the meantime. It's the hardest because figuring out future profitability isn't easy, particularly for Internet stocks, whose long-term potential is still largely guesswork. And it's the most important because valuation is the underlying principle of all investing. Ultimately, the stock market is a mechanism for determining the appropriate value of a company. In the long term, it's proven to be a pretty reliable mechanism. In the short term, it frequently makes mistakes. The smartest investor is the one who can recognize and buy stocks trading at less than their true value and sell them at or above their true value. But if you have no idea what that underlying value is, you're flying blind.

A few points about valuation: First, the same company can be worth different things to different people, depending on their time horizon and their appetite for risk. In other words, if my investing horizon is short—say, three years—I might be willing to pay more for what looks like a safer investment, but therefore accept a somewhat lower return, than someone who's socking away money for thirty years and who therefore can afford to take on more risks.

Second, valuation is not a science, particularly for stocks as early in their life cycles and with as much open-ended opportunity as those in the Internet sector. In calculating the discounted present value of future earnings, for example, you need to make guesses not just about how much a company will earn down the road but about how much other investors might be willing to pay for those profits, and what your money could be doing in the meantime. Be prepared to think in terms of ballparks and ranges.

Third, Net stocks aren't cheap by virtually every traditional means of analysis—and even by some not-so-traditional means. They never have been cheap, and they're not likely to become cheap in the foreseeable future. In fact, if a stock does look cheap, beware. For the most part, stocks trading for a couple of dollars a share, and with total market values in the tens of millions of dollars rather than the billions, are there because the market has determined their chances of success to be small. If they fail and you lose all your money, the least expensive investment can turn out to be the costliest. By and large, you get what you pay for, and the companies with the best track records, which are accorded the best chances of success, don't come cheap. As Internet analyst Henry Blodget of Merrill Lynch writes, "Over the long haul, it is difficult to generate first-rate returns by investing in second-rate companies." (Remember, by the way, that the price of an individual share of stock isn't cheap or expensive in a vacuum. A $3 share of company X isn't necessarily "cheaper" than a $50 share of company Y. To figure out the total value of a company—what's known as the "market capitalization"—multiply the price of each share by the number of shares outstanding.)

If valuation is contingent on profit potential, then the first thing we need to do is determine how to estimate a company's potential profit. There are a number of more or less complicated ways of accomplishing this, but the quickest way to get a rough idea is to follow these three easy steps:

1. Determine the size of the overall market the company is going after.

2. Multiply that by the company's market share (current or expected) to determine its potential revenue.

3. Multiply the potential revenue by the amount of money the company earns on each dollar of revenue (the "profit margin"). The result is the potential profit.

Once you've figured out the potential profit, you're halfway to figuring out a fair value for the company. The next step is to determine the company's "price-to-earnings ratio," which is simply a measure of how the stock price relates to the company's profits. Take the company's market value, divide that number by its potential profit, and you have the P/E ratio. (Alternately, you can figure out the company's earnings per share by dividing the overall earnings by the number of shares of stock outstanding, and then figure out the P/E ratio by dividing the price of a single share of stock by the EPS. Either way, you should end up with the same result.) Comparing the P/E ratio of one company with the P/E ratios of other companies in its sector, or with the P/E ratio of the market as a whole, is a commonly used method of figuring out whether a stock is cheap or expensive on a *relative* basis.

Relative valuation is important because it can help you gauge whether a stock is trading at an unsustainable premium to the rest of the market (or its peer group) or at a deep discount. Generally speaking, stocks command premiums only when they're growing significantly faster than the market (or their peers). (That's one reason Net stocks are so expensive—the companies are growing, at least in terms of revenues, at breakneck speed.) But over the very long term, stocks tend to fall into line with the "market multiple"—the multiple of earnings that investors are willing to pay to own a stock.

Some investors might stop right here. If, for example, they do the math and find that Yahoo!, the Web portal giant, is trading at 140 times next year's expected earnings versus 100 times those earnings for a more mature market-leading technology company such as Cisco Systems—and just 30 times earnings for the stock market as a whole—they might rule out Yahoo! as too pricey. This is not necessarily a bad way of doing things. Other investors might take the analysis a step further and say that they'd be willing to pay up for Yahoo! since it's such a fast-growing company. In other words, if Yahoo!'s earnings are growing at 50 percent a year, then in four years the company's earnings will be five times what they are today. Such a company, then, is presumably worth a higher multiple of those earnings than one that has the exact same earnings today but is growing at just 10 percent a year.

Now the question becomes: How much are you willing to pay for that kind of growth? This is where the analysis becomes trickier. To begin with, we need to come up with an appropriate number to discount those expected future earnings back to their present value. In other words, how much are you willing to pay today for $1 worth of earnings five years from now? The "discount rate" is essentially a way of factoring into the price of a stock your own return requirements, and the risk of holding that stock, versus what else your money could be doing in the meantime.

The best way of seeing how all this works in practice is to return to the Yahoo! example, courtesy of Merrill Lynch. Yahoo!'s business model was discussed at length in Chapter Three, but for now—since we're focusing simply on its stock price—it's important to remember only that Yahoo! makes most of its money from selling advertising. Merrill estimates that the total amount spent on advertising and direct marketing in the United States in the year 2005 will hit $250 billion, while the total amount spent globally will hit $600 billion. Of that, Merrill estimates that between 10 and 15 percent will be spent advertising on-line. If Yahoo! were to win all those advertising dollars—an impossible task—its total "addressable market" would be somewhere between $30 billion and $60 billion. As of the year 2000, Yahoo! controlled between 10 and 15 percent of the on-line advertising market. At those levels, given the size of the on-line advertising market as a whole, we come up with potential revenues for the company of between $3 billion and $9 billion in the year 2005. That's a huge range, of course, but if we take the middle of the range, we come up with a reasonable best-guess number of $6 billion.

As of the year 2000, Yahoo!'s bottom-line profit margin was in the neighborhood of 28 percent. That means that for every dollar of revenue it took in, the company earned 28 cents after operating expenses and taxes. Merrill thinks this number can grow to 35 percent by the year 2005, as Yahoo! grows bigger and achieves better economies of scale. At that rate, Yahoo!'s profit on $6 billion of revenue would be in the neighborhood of $2 billion.

At the time Merrill conducted this analysis, Yahoo! was trading at 140 times its expected earnings for the following year. As we've seen, that's extremely rich—several times the forward earnings multiple of the market as a whole and even ahead of market-leading companies such as Cisco Systems, which commanded a multiple of 100 times next year's earnings. If we assume that Yahoo!'s multiple shrinks to a still rich Cisco-like level by 2004 and we estimate $2 billion in 2005 earnings, multiplying 100 times $2 billion gives us a market capitalization of $200 billion. Dividing that by the total number of shares of Yahoo! stock outstanding gives us a share price of more than of $300 in 2004.

Now comes the key question: How much is $300 in 2004 worth today? In other words, how much do we need Yahoo! to return each year to offset the risk of holding this stock and the risk that the company won't achieve our growth targets, as well as the alternative places we could put our money in the meantime? Let's say, for the sake of argument, that we require a 20 percent annual return (that's about twice the average annual return of the stock market as a whole over the very long term). The formula to discount a projected price into current dollars is to divide the projected price by the required return taken to the multiple of the number of periods involved. In other words, in this case it is $300 divided by $(1.2)^3$. That gives us a share price, in the year 2001, of $174. In other words, if we can buy Yahoo! today at $174 or less, the stock is attractively priced given our assumptions about the future.

There are a few things to keep in mind. First of all, we should recognize just how many assumptions we're making. If we're wrong, $174 might seem fantastically overpriced. For example, if Yahoo! takes in revenues of only $3 billion in 2005, instead of $6 billion (either because the market doesn't grow as fast as Merrill's projections or because Yahoo!'s market share shrinks), and if its profit margins stay at 28 percent instead of growing to 35 percent, as Merrill anticipates they will, then Yahoo!'s earnings in 2005 will be closer to $840 million than $2 billion. That gives us a share price in 2004 of just $133, less than half the $300 our other calculations suggest. And that gives us a 2001 value of just $77 a share. What's more, if Yahoo!'s slowing growth under those circumstances leads the market to value it at a lower multiple, say 50 times forward earnings, rather than the premium of 100 times earnings we're anticipating, that number would be even lower: just $39 a share. On the other hand, if Yahoo! exceeds expectations, and if it expands into new lines of business, as appears likely, our numbers could prove conservative. At the high end of our projections, with $9 billion in revenues and a 35 percent profit margin, Yahoo! would be worth $273 in 2001. Also, don't forget how big an impact our required return rate has on this calculation. If we require just a 10 percent return, we'd be willing to pay $238 for that $2 billion in 2005 earnings, not the $174 our 20 percent return yielded.

All of this raises a question that has nagged at Internet investors since the dawn of Internet investing: What if you perform all these calculations and all this analysis, and the stock still seems expensive? Does that mean you should rule out buying it? Not necessarily. In some cases, given how early we still are in the evolution of the industry and how quickly some of these companies are changing, you might simply want to take on faith that a company will "grow into" the valuation the market has bestowed on it. In Yahoo!'s case, for example, our initial analysis completely ignored sources of revenue besides advertising, including commerce or other lines of business we can't even think of, that Yahoo! may pursue. If we are convinced, as many investors are, that Yahoo! has a first-class management team and that its status as the world's leading Internet portal will give it advantages in entering new business areas, we might go ahead and buy the stock even at a price that's higher than what our analysis would suggest.

Certainly, this is a high-risk approach, and one that isn't advisable for all investors. Grandma, for example, probably shouldn't be using her retirement savings to buy shares of a richly valued dot com on the belief that it might someday grow into a value that seems preposterous right now. But other investors, with many years to go yet before their retirement, might decide that putting a small portion of their savings in such investments is a risk that's worth taking—and maybe even silly not to take.

All this becomes even more important when looking at companies that, unlike Yahoo!, are losing money. Take the best known of these companies, Amazon.com—a company that its own founder, Jeff Bezos, has called "famously unprofitable." As of late 2000, its annual losses were in the many millions of dollars. But its revenues are expected to hit $3.5 billion for all of 2001, several times their level just three years earlier. For a company like this, which has no earnings track record on which we can base assumptions about future earnings growth, we simply need to make our analysis that much more speculative—realizing that our conclusions are that much more flimsy and our investment that much riskier. Returning to the back-of-the-envelope analysis provided by Merrill Lynch, we can guesstimate that on-line retailing will eventually account for 10 percent of the $2.6 trillion U.S. retailing market, or about $260 billion. Amazon's stated aim is to become the on-line location where shoppers can find anything they want to buy under the sun. If we assume that Amazon can one day account for 30 percent of that on-line shopping volume (an aggressive assumption, to be sure, but not inconceivable given Amazon's current dominance of the on-line businesses it's in), we come up with potential revenues of $78 billion. And if we then assume a rather narrow net profit margin of, say, 5 percent (again, more than Amazon has ever made, since its recent profit margins have been negative), we come up with potential annual profits of nearly $4 billion. Taken at a market multiple of 45 or 50 times earnings, we come up with a potential market capitalization approaching $200 billion, many times Amazon's current level. Of course, it could take many years for Amazon to hit these kinds of numbers (if it ever gets there at all). In the nearer term, Merrill's Mr. Blodget has estimated that Amazon could hit revenues of just under $20 billion and earnings of $1.5 billion by the year 2005. That implies earnings per share of just under $3, which at a market multiple implies a stock price of $150 in the year 2004. Discounted back at a 20 percent annual return, that results in a 2001 stock price of $87 per share. But perhaps, because our numbers are so speculative, and because Amazon hasn't yet demonstrated the ability to earn a profit—or to dominate so many different retailing categories—we require an even higher rate of return. That would imply a lower current stock price. Or perhaps we're willing to take more on faith and recognize that our estimates don't take into account potential growth overseas, and we'll buy the stock even at a price that seems high, aware that we're taking on a sizable risk by doing so.

Basket Weaving

While picking and valuing individual stocks is important, an equally important aspect of successful Internet investing—or any form of investing, for that matter—is deciding how much of your portfolio to allocate to various types of stocks. What makes this particularly difficult is that there are really only two absolutes. First, just as your investment portfolio should include a mix of various types of assets—stocks, bonds, cash, and perhaps even real estate or commodities—so, too, should your stock portfolio include exposure to a mix of different industries and sectors. Similarly, just as your investment portfolio should never be devoid of stocks entirely, so too should your stock portfolio never be devoid of exposure to Internet or technology stocks. But how much exposure, and to what sort of Internet or technology stocks, is a strictly personal choice.

Three points should factor into your decision. First, what are your age and your investment horizon? In other words, how soon are you likely to need the money you're putting away now? If your horizon is short, say less than five years, then you should probably have only minimal exposure to the tech sector, keeping in mind that tech stocks tend to be richly priced and volatile relative to the broader market. (You don't want to buy at a relative peak and find yourself needing to sell at a relative trough just a few years later.) If, on the other hand, your horizon is twenty or thirty years, you may want to put a bigger chunk of your money into tech stocks, knowing that you can afford some nearer-term volatility in exchange for the potential for longer-term profits. At the same time, don't forget that a key principle of investing is never to put your money in a place where it's going to keep you up at night. You know yourself best. If you are the type of person who can't tear himself away from the minute-to-minute gyrations of his portfolio, no matter what the experts tell you about socking your money away and forgetting about it, then you probably should keep that in mind when allocating your investments. Tech stocks *will* gyrate. And if that's going to keep you up at night, then no matter what your investment horizon, you should probably put a bit less into the tech sector than another investor who's better able to invest and forget about it.

Second, to what extent are you dependent on the income your investments will generate? In other words, even if you don't need to touch your principal anytime soon but you do need your investments to generate a certain amount of cash, you should probably keep your exposure to the Internet and tech sector limited. Tech stocks, pretty much across the board, do not pay dividends. Virtually all tech companies plow their profits right back into growth, or research and development, in order not to get sidelined or caught off guard by nimbler competitors. (And clearly, money-losing Internet companies have no profits with which to pay dividends in the first place!) The bottom line: Money placed into tech and Internet stocks should be money that you can afford to forget about for a while.

Third, keep in mind that, whether or not you know it, you probably have some exposure to the Internet already. If you're invested in any sort of broad mutual funds that track the market, or even if you're invested in any of a number of major companies that are dipping their toes in or benefiting from the growth of the Net, then you should count those investments toward your Internet allocation. As we've seen, for example, the Standard & Poor's 500 stock index now includes two major Internet companies in its ranks: AOL Time Warner and Yahoo!. And because the S&P is a market cap–weighted index—meaning that companies with bigger market values factor more heavily into its performance—those two companies, with their large market values, play a bigger role in the index than if they were just two names out of five hundred equally weighted stocks. Specifically, as of late 2000, AOL and Yahoo! together accounted for roughly 1 percent of the index's performance. That means that any mutual fund you own that tracks the S&P 500 probably has about 1 percent of its assets invested in those two stocks at any one time (depending on how their market value shifts in relation to the rest of the stocks in the group).

As we've mentioned, beyond the "pure" Internet companies such as AOL and Yahoo!, there are dozens upon dozens of other companies that derive a substantial portion of their business from Internet-related activities or indirectly from the growth of the Net.

Microsoft, Intel, Hewlett-Packard, and IBM, for example, are all heavily involved in the Internet, selling much of the hardware and software that powers the Net and selling many of their goods and services on-line. Similarly, AT&T and WorldCom both derive substantial revenues from the Internet traffic that flows over the "pipes" they own. Together, as of late 2000, these companies accounted for about 1.25 percent of the S&P 500, while Microsoft, Intel, IBM, and AT&T accounted for more than 13 percent of the performance of the Dow Jones Industrial Average. Thus, if you're invested in any of these companies, you need to consider that investment as part of your Internet and technology portfolio. And if you're invested in any of these stocks on top of investments in broader funds that own these stocks, you should add those allocations together when determining your overall exposure. (If I own 100 shares of AT&T, for example, and 100 shares of a fund that tracks the S&P 500 and is 1 percent exposed to AT&T, then my total ownership of AT&T is actually 101 shares, rather than the 100 shares I own outright.)

Once you've decided how much exposure to Internet stocks you desire and determined how much exposure you already have, you need to figure out how you actually want to obtain that exposure. This, too, is a two-step process. Step one is determining whether you're more comfortable investing *directly* in the Net, in names such as AOL and Yahoo!, or *indirectly*, in names such as AT&T and WorldCom, or even FedEx and UPS. The more conservative you are and the shorter your time horizon, the more heavily your portfolio should be weighted toward indirect Net investments and perhaps some Internet infrastructure stocks. Similarly, the more aggressive you are and the longer your time horizon, the more you can afford to be exposed to the purer Net stocks and those with more virtual business models.

Step two is determining whether you want to choose individual stocks yourself or simply choose mutual funds and leave the stock picking up to a fund manager (or some combination of the two). For most investors (notwithstanding everything you're reading in this book), the best answer is simply to leave the stock picking up to the experts. That means choosing the funds that best suit your needs and investment style and that have the best track records, and simply monitoring their performance periodically. But even for investors who decide they want to select their own individual stocks, the key to success is to diversify among a basket of names within different subsectors of the Internet economy, creating an individual little mutual fund of sorts. This kind of diversification—a few business-to-consumer names, a few business-to-business names, several infrastructure companies, and a medley of Internet proxy investments (in companies that benefit from the growth of the Net without being Internet companies themselves)—maximizes your chances of being exposed to the long-term winners and minimizes the chances that you'll suffer unduly should you end up invested in a loser. And it's particularly important in a sector as new and evolving as the Internet, where separating the winners from the losers is still very much a game of making educated guesses.

Along those lines, it's worth noting that venture capitalists, who invest in high-risk start-ups for a living, expect that for every one of their investments that performs spectacularly, several will perform only modestly well, while several others will go out of business altogether. One "ten-bagger"—a company that returns its initial investment tenfold—can offset a lot of duds. Internet investors can do very well adopting a similar approach, which is why a basket investment strategy makes sense. If you choose ten Net stocks to invest in and three go out of business, you can still achieve a respectable overall return as long as several of the others deliver decent performances and one turns into a home run. Put a bit differently, not every investment needs to be a winner as long as some of them are.

CHAPTER EIGHT

Leaving the Tough Stuff to Others

Incubators and Mutual Funds

I F THERE'S ONE THING the last seven chapters should have made clear, it's that investing—not just Internet investing, but any investing—isn't easy. There's work involved, particularly if you're going to pick individual stocks. You need to find quality companies, learn about them, and do a fair amount of homework before putting your money behind them. There are, of course, professional stockbrokers who'll be more than happy to do the grunt work for you. But farming your assets out to a broker isn't cheap, and it takes away some of the fun of controlling your own destiny. Then, too, as the commercial for E*TRADE points out, if the brokers are so smart, how come they're still working?

There are shortcuts, however, in the form of individual investments that, in one fell swoop, put your money to work in a myriad of different companies. In this chapter, we'll take a look at two different forms of these investments: Internet "incubators," which are essentially holding companies that make a living helping other Internet companies get off the ground, and mutual funds, massive pools of money that invest in the stocks of publicly traded companies. Think of this, then, as the chapter for people who want all the benefits of being an Internet investor without all the bother!

Company Snapshot: CMGI

At a Glance
Ticker symbol: CMGI
Founded: 1968
Went public: 1994
Fiscal 2000 revenue: $898 million (year ended July 31)
Revenue growth rate (vs. 1999): 382%
Fiscal 2000 losses: $1.36 billion (year ended July 31)
Profit growth rate (vs. 1999): NA
Key management: David Wetherell, Chairman and CEO

Founded as a distributor of mailing lists and marketer of college textbooks, CMGI (formerly known as College Marketing Group) was taken over by entrepreneur David Wetherell in a leveraged buyout in 1986 and gradually transformed into an "incubator" of Internet companies. The company's strategy is to invest in a broad array of Internet start-ups, nurture them with assistance in areas such as human resources, public relations, and accounting, and encourage them to feed business to one another. Ultimately, CMGI takes the companies public, profiting from its investments by selling shares on the capital markets.

The strategy worked brilliantly during the height of the Internet stock mania, as CMGI spun off companies such as Lycos, Engage, and Mail.com. CMGI became one of the best-performing stocks of the 1990s, and Wetherell earned a reputation as a brilliant investor and an Internet visionary—as well as a personal net worth in the billions of dollars. But CMGI's fortunes soured in the year 2000, as the market for Internet stocks tanked and its own stock followed suit. The company determined to transform itself into an operator of Internet companies rather than simply an investor, though Wetherell claimed this was, in fact, what he'd been doing all along. CMGI was reorganized into six areas of focus, of which venture capital was one. Others included interactive marketing (where CMGI competes with players such as DoubleClick), portals and search technology, fulfillment operations (the back-end picking, packing, and shipping required to allow e-commerce companies to distribute products), infrastructure and enabling technologies, and consulting (which CMGI terms Internet Professional Services). The goal was to demonstrate to investors that CMGI could develop a reliable, recurring revenue stream—and ultimately an operating profit—without relying so heavily on the whims of the public capital markets.

Mommy, Where Do Baby Dot Coms Come From?

The term "Internet incubator" conjures up the image of a warm, cozy place where fledgling Web sites are nurtured into full-grown Web companies, like baby chickens. That image isn't totally off base. Companies may come to incubators in various stages of development, though often they show up with nothing more than an idea for a business. The goal of the incubator is to help take these start-ups from inception, or shortly thereafter, to maturity as independent, publicly traded concerns. In some cases, that may involve little more than providing the money that's needed to execute an idea, and in those cases incubators aren't functionally all that different from ordinary venture capital firms, which make their living by funding new companies. But incubators may go much further than that, providing everything from office space, desks, and computers to professional services, advice, and connections. And while many venture capital firms also encourage their portfolio companies to work together and provide one another with business, this process is, in theory at least, much more formalized for incubators. Thus, an incubator with investments in an on-line retailer, an Internet consulting firm, and a wireless software company may encourage the retailer to use the consulting firm's services and the wireless company's software, rather than the services of potential rivals, in the hope that each of the companies will help promote success at each of the others. This approach resembles that of the Japanese *keiretsu*—a tightly knit circle of companies that do business with one another and frequently have ownership stakes in one another. And although the power of the *keiretsu* has waned in Japan, the concept has proved particularly suitable to the Internet. The Net, after all, has led to the creation of hundreds of start-up companies, all requiring many of the same basic services. And fledgling Web sites craving traffic have found that a great way to obtain that traffic is to have it directed their way by other Web sites.

Let's take a real-life example. Raging Bull is an Internet community site focused on investing that was created by some Duke University undergraduates in their dorm room. As the upstart Web site grew in popularity, it attracted the attention of David Wetherell, chairman of a company called CMGI, one of the first Internet incubators. Wetherell contacted the students, who within days were in his Andover, Massachusetts, office, presenting CMGI with a hastily crafted business plan. Within a few weeks, CMGI had provided Raging Bull with several million dollars in funding, set up the company in fully furnished office space at CMGI's headquarters, and provided the expertise of CMGI's human resources department to help the young college students interview and hire dozens of employees. Ultimately, Raging Bull was merged into another CMGI property, AltaVista, to become the financial community section of the AltaVista portal. And later it was sold to another CMGI-funded company, TerraLycos, parent of the Lycos portal site. The combination helps Raging Bull by steering Lycos's millions of portal users to its site. And it helps Lycos by attracting a particularly "sticky" type of user, who tends to spend all kinds of time chatting about investments with other Raging Bull participants.

Like venture capitalists, incubators generally make their money in one of two ways: either by selling their progeny off to other companies or by taking them public and unloading their private stakes on the public markets, usually at huge markups to the cost of the original investments. CMGI, for example, became noteworthy for two major successes: investments of several million dollars in two start-ups, Lycos and GeoCities, a community site, that ultimately assumed values of several billion dollars when the sites went public and were later sold. But like venture capitalists, incubators operate on the philosophy that many, if not most, of the start-ups they invest in will fail. That's OK if, every once in a while, you're able to take a $4 million investment in a company such as Lycos and turn it into a stake worth $4 billion. Both venture capitalists and incubators seek to achieve annual returns on their investments that are two or even three times higher than the 10 percent or so offered by the broader stock market over the very long term, to compensate for the high risks that go along with their strategy.

Company Snapshot: Internet Capital Group

At a Glance
Ticker symbol: ICGE
Founded: 1996
Went public: 1999
2000 revenue: $21.7 million (through fiscal Q3)
Revenue growth rate (vs. 1999): 46.6%
2000 losses: $98.7 million
Profit growth rate (vs. 1999): NA
Key management: Walter Buckley, President and CEO

Itself the product of a publicly traded Internet incubator—Safeguard Scientifics—Internet Capital Group was created to help nurture and develop other Internet companies focused on the emerging business-to-business arena. In this sense, an investment in ICGE is a bet not just on the Internet sector generally or on the ability of ICGE's management team to spot and invest in promising Internet companies, but on the prospects of the B2B e-commerce subsector specifically. Within that subsector, ICGE's focus has been on developing marketplaces for the trading of goods and services among companies, as well as companies that develop the software to operate these types of exchanges and consulting firms that specialize in B2B e-commerce. The goal is to focus on industries—"verticals" in Internet parlance—that can be made much more efficient by moving them on-line.

For a time, ICGE met with spectacular success, including most notably with the initial public offering of VerticalNet, one of the more successful B2B exchanges. ICGE's own stock was also one of the star performers of 1999, though its spectacular ascent turned into a spectacular descent the following year as Internet stocks generally, and B2B stocks in particular, fell out of favor with many investors. At that point, ICGE's investments in a broad swath of B2B exchanges—from e-Chemicals to eCredit.com to Cyber-Crop.com—began to look more like liabilities than assets.

What's In It for Me?

For a long time, the outsized returns achieved by the most successful venture capitalists were off limits to ordinary investors. To this day, most of the funds raise their investment dollars from institutional investors, such as pension funds and endowments, as well as from a handful of wealthy individuals—in part because of a belief that these "sophisticated" investors understand the risks of venture capital investing, and in part because it's easier logistically to raise and administer large sums of money from just a few big investors. But the move of several incubators, such as CMGI, to raise money on the public markets has opened up the risks and rewards of venture capital to ordinary investors as well.

What are those risks and rewards? The rewards are twofold: first, the ability, through a single investment, to own stakes in a diversified set of companies; and second, the ability to obtain those stakes at cheap, pre-IPO prices. That diversification means that incubators represent almost an agnostic bet on the growth of the Internet. An investment in an incubator company, after all, is a bet not on any one technology or any one business model, but on a number of different technologies and business models, any one of which might succeed. (A caveat: some incubators do tend to focus on a particular subsector of the Internet economy, meaning that an investment in such a company is a bet on the growth of that subsector, rather than on the Internet economy as a whole.)

One risk that accompanies those rewards relates to copycat incubators that have popped up, hoping to mimic the phenomenal early success of the original players, like CMGI, Softbank, and Safeguard Scientifics. These newcomers tend to flood the market with capital and swarm over would-be Internet entrepreneurs. Amid the stock market's euphoria, venture capital dollars aimed at the Internet totaled a little more than $30 billion in the first half of 2000, up from $28 billion for all of 1999, and accounting for 85 percent of all venture capital investments for the period, according to VentureOne, a venture capital research firm. Though this pace slowed considerably during the second half of 2000, the effect of such a capital glut can be to drive up the cost of the best early-stage investments. As more money chases after these investments, some start-ups that don't deserve it receive funding, while others are awarded higher valuations than they deserve. And remember: just because an incubator has investments in many different companies, that doesn't mean any of them will succeed or return enough to offset the losses sustained by those that flop.

Aside from execution risks, there are market risks. Even the best incubators are sensitive to depressed capital markets, because their profitability is contingent on their ability to sell off their stakes in the public markets. If they can't take companies public, it's difficult to earn back the money they've invested. As a result, in down markets, such as the one that began in the spring of 2000, the downside on an incubator's stock is often exaggerated compared to other stocks. (This, too, can have a domino effect, closing the funding door to start-ups with worthy ideas.)

What's It Worth?

Determining the value of an incubator is a tricky proposition. Unlike a traditional operating company—which runs its business directly—incubators don't have regular streams of revenues and profits. For the most part, their profits come in fits and starts, when they sell portions of their holdings. That income is nonrecurring, meaning that once recognized, it doesn't regenerate. For example, when a traditional operating company, such as Cisco, sells a product—say, a router—not only does it recognize the proceeds from that sale, it also continues to own and operate the infrastructure needed to keep producing and selling more routers in the future. Not so for an incubator. Once it sells its stake in a company, that stake is history and creates no opportunity for future profits. The incubator may take some of the proceeds of that sale and invest them in other investment opportunities. But each time it does that, it's essentially starting from scratch, and its subsequent investments may or may not pay off.

This kind of structure gives incubators an unusual degree of control over when to recognize profits. For investors, though, it means an incubator's value can't be determined from its expected operating income, as it is with most other companies. Instead, the value of an incubator is the sum of the value of all of its investments—and even the best incubator won't make a profitable investment if you pay more for the stock than its component investments are worth. But determining that value can be next to impossible. Wall Street analysts make occasional attempts at piecing together valuations, adding up the value of an incubator's holdings in publicly traded companies with a best-guess assessment of their private holdings to come up with an overall value. These estimates can be useful guideposts, but that's all they are. For investors considering a bet on incubators, the most important indicator of their potential is their track record. In the absence of much other information, it's a relatively safe assumption that incubators with a successful history of picking winners are more likely to pick winning investments in the future than incubators without that history, if only because of the lessons they've learned and their knowledge of the industry. What's more, success in the venture capital business tends to breed more success. Start-ups tend to seek out venture capitalists with the strongest track records, which means that the best venture capitalists tend to have their pick of the best new business ideas. Still, this approach is hardly foolproof.

An Explosion of Funds

Along with the explosion in venture capital dollars chasing after Internet start-ups, the late 1990s witnessed an explosion in mutual funds chasing after the stocks of publicly traded Internet companies. There are now literally hundreds of mutual funds that target high-tech stocks, with many of these focused on Internet stocks. Between 1994 and 2000, the number of mutual funds focused on technology stocks more than quadrupled, to eighty-three, with the assets under their control skyrocketing from $6.5 billion to nearly $140 billion, according to Morningstar. In addition, many growth-oriented funds—generally defined as those that seek out companies with revenues or profits growing at a faster rate than the broader market—took on an Internet bent as the Internet sector became the epicenter of the market's growth. Meanwhile, many broader funds now include healthy allocations to Internet stocks, particularly following the addition of AOL and Yahoo! to the Standard & Poor's 500 stock index. As of late 2000, those two names together accounted for roughly 1 percent of the index, while technology and software names altogether accounted for 7 percent.

Mutual Fund Snapshot: Baron iOpportunity Fund

At a Glance
Established: 2000
Assets under management: $202 million
2000 return: −39.0%
Return since inception: −39.0%
Fund managers: Mitch Rubin

The notion of a value-oriented Internet mutual fund seemed oxymoronic, even laughable, when the Baron iOpportunity Fund was established in early 2000, just before the mania for Internet stocks reached its height. But times and stock valuations change, and the Baron fund's value-driven approach seemed prescient only a few months later, even if its year 2000 performance suffered from the tech selloff.

The fund's manager insists on paying reasonable prices for companies with attainable profitability targets. And the fund takes a long-term approach—content to wait a couple of years for an investment to pay off, as long as there's a likelihood it will pay off in a big way. According to its manager, the "i" in the iOpportunity Fund stands not just for Internet but also for information technology, interactive communication, and information systems infrastructure. The fund seeks investments in a broad spectrum of companies that stand to benefit from the opportunities and efficiencies created by the Internet and related technologies, without limiting itself to pure-play Internet companies alone.

What does that mean in practice? The fund's holdings have, at times, included Heidrick & Struggles International, an executive recruitment firm that has an on-line headhunting subsidiary, as well as Comcast, a cable television company that in addition to its core business offers the prospect of growth in the high-speed Internet access business, and the Hotel Reservations Network, a hotel room–booking service that derives much, though not all, of its business on-line.

That broad variety of funds investing in Internet stocks presents Internet investors with a variety of different ways to approach the sector. Ultraconservative investors may be satisfied with the smattering of large-cap Net and technology stocks they're exposed to through an S&P index fund. Other investors may wish to take on additional risk, either by investing in a broad growth fund that includes some Net stocks or by putting money in a sector fund targeted more precisely at Net stocks alone.

Let's pause here to define some terms. While not all growth funds are Internet funds, all funds that focus on Net stocks are, by definition, growth-oriented, since just about every company in the sector has revenues, if not profits, that are growing at a faster rate than the market as a whole. Some Net funds are even "aggressive growth" funds, in that they zero in on the fastest-growing, and frequently most speculative, Net stocks. Similarly, Net funds are, by definition, *not* value funds, according to the generally accepted definition of that term, in that they don't focus on stocks that trade at a discount to the broader market. The simple reason: there *are* no Net stocks that trade at a discount to the broader market, when measured using standard price-to-earnings ratios. There are some

Net funds that have tried to take a valuelike approach by focusing on Net stocks that trade at a *relative* discount to *other* Net stocks. Some traditional value-oriented funds have also dabbled in the Net sector, picking through the mass of richly priced Net stocks to try to find those that are less richly priced. Often, these funds have simply tried to add juice to an investment strategy that, by and large, was a dud during the late 1990s.

Within the Net sector, there are two different types of funds: sectorwide funds, which pick stocks from all the various branches of the Internet, and subsector-specific funds, which focus exclusively on individual Internet subsectors. Among the first category, the Munder NetNet Fund is a prime example. One of the first Internet mutual funds and now the largest, the NetNet Fund includes a mix of companies in each of the three big Internet subcategories: consumer-oriented Web sites, business-to-business companies, and infrastructure firms. As of late 2000, the fund (which is closed to new investors) had stakes in companies ranging from Amazon.com to Ariba to Cisco Systems. But the NetNet Fund doesn't stop there. It also includes a smattering of Net proxy stocks, such as Dell Computer and World-Com. And it has, at times, included bricks-and-mortar companies, such as The Gap, that have an on-line presence. In short, the NetNet Fund is focused on the Internet, broadly defined. As the fund itself puts it, it "invests in the stocks of companies positioned to benefit from the growth of the Internet." That includes not just technology companies but "companies across all sectors that are poised to use the Internet to their advantage." Notably, the fund does not limit itself to companies whose business is *mostly* or *exclusively* Internet-related.

As a result of its focus, the NetNet Fund is substantially riskier than a broader fund—say, one pegged to the S&P 500. According to a risk analysis conducted by Morningstar, the mutual fund–rating concern, the NetNet Fund is 81% riskier than the average domestic stock fund, meaning there's a substantially higher chance of losing money on the Munder fund. The hope is that the fund's returns will make that risk worth taking. In fact, according to Morningstar, the NetNet Fund's performance in the three years from 1998 through 2000 exceeded those of the average domestic stock fund by nearly 1,100 percent, though the fund began to underperform in late 2000, as the tech-stock selloff worsened.

Mutual Fund Snapshot: Jacob Internet Fund

At a Glance
Established: 1999
Assets under management: $127 million
2000 return: −79.1%
Return Since Inception: −78.9%
Fund Manager: Ryan Jacob

Once a darling of the Internet mutual fund world, the boyish-looking Ryan Jacob rose to stardom as manager of the Internet Fund, which amassed a return of more than 230 percent during the year and a half Jacob was responsible for it. Jacob left the Internet Fund in the summer of 1999, determined to use his newfound fame to start his own mutual fund company—and leading to a squabble with his ex-employer over who could claim the credit for the fund's performance. As it turned out, though the Internet Fund's performance did sag after Jacob's departure, the early performance of his own fund didn't exactly follow the white-hot trail he had previously blazed.

The Jacob Internet Fund's strategy is to invest in two key subsectors of the Internet economy: the business-to-consumer sector, where it focuses on content providers and e-commerce firms, and the infrastructure sector, where it targets communications firms and access providers. As it happens, while both subsectors fell on hard times right around the time the fund was launched, it was the business-to-consumer sector, in which the fund was most heavily concentrated, that was hit the hardest, accounting for its disappointing performance.

Looking forward, the fund's emphasis is on small to medium-sized companies. This approach earns it a distinction as a particularly aggressive—and risky—mutual fund, even within a universe of aggressive and risky funds.

At the same time, the Munder fund is also less risky—but may offer less potential reward—than a more aggressively oriented Net fund, such as one that avoids bricks-and-mortar companies altogether and focuses exclusively on pure-play Net companies. Consider, for example, the Jacob Internet Fund, which according to its marketing materials targets "Internet-centric businesses," as opposed to companies that simply benefit from the Net. Although the Jacob fund is too young for Morningstar's numbers-based risk analysis, the ratings concern's analysts call the fund "very, very risky." And it's not hard to see why. Among the fund's holdings, as of late 2000, were content sites such as iVillage and MarketWatch.com, portals such as StarMedia Network, and commerce sites such as eBay and Priceline. Some of those companies are also in the Munder fund, but the Jacob fund is less diversified, with just twenty-five different stocks in its portfolio, one quarter the number the NetNet Fund holds. The Jacob fund also tends to target smaller, earlier-stage companies with an average market capitalization of under $1 billion, according to Morningstar, compared with Munder's average market cap of more than $13 billion. These younger companies may have more room to grow than those in the NetNet Fund's portfolio, meaning that the potential return on investment is greater. But they also have less of a commanding market presence and are more likely to fail than the more established companies in the Munder fund.

Potentially even riskier—and perhaps more rewarding—than a fund targeting pure-play Net stocks is one that delves within the Internet sector to target particular categories of Net companies, such as commerce, infrastructure, or business to business. For example, the Firsthand Funds group offers an e-Commerce Fund that invests in companies that provide the infrastructure that allows retailers to operate on-line. The fund doesn't include any on-line retailers themselves but does include consultants and software vendors such as VeriSign, BEA Systems, and Interliant. The e-Commerce Fund's focus means that it's better positioned than the Munder fund to benefit from a boom in on-line commerce stocks. At the same time, a sell-off in this narrow category would inflict relatively greater damage on the e-Commerce Fund's returns. (Like the Jacob fund, the e-Commerce Fund isn't old enough to earn an official Morningstar rating. But Morningstar's analysts concur with this analysis, terming the fund's focus "ultranarrow" and likely to produce "an extremely volatile ride.")

How Do You Say "Internet" in German?

While many Internet-oriented mutual funds include a few companies based outside the United States among their holdings, a few funds target these foreign stocks specifically. Munder, for example, offers an International NetNet Fund that, according to its prospectus, will invest at least 65 percent of its assets in the stocks of foreign companies in Internet-related businesses. Similarly, the Monument Funds Group offers a EuroNet Fund that focuses exclusively on Internet companies based in Europe. These types of funds offer an opportunity to diversify beyond U.S.-based companies and invest in the expected growth of the Net abroad. But such investments come with their own set of risks.

First, even though Internet usage is expected to increase faster in coming years outside the United States than it will in the United States, many of the companies that dominate the global Internet are still likely to be American. eBay, for example, is the worldwide leader in person-to-person auctions, despite the competition it faces in Europe from London-based QXL. (In Japan, the auction leader is none other than eBay's U.S.-based rival, Yahoo!.) As a result, investors in the foreign rivals to these American giants may be missing out on the players that are actually best positioned to capitalize on the Net's international growth and unintentionally putting their money behind second-tier players instead.

Second, the fact that a company is based outside the United States doesn't mean it's immune to the trading patterns affecting U.S. stocks. A sell-off in technology stocks in the United States, for example, is likely to follow, or be followed by, a corresponding sell-off in technology stocks in Europe and the Far East. What's more, many foreign Internet firms trade both in their home countries and in the United States. Returning to our previous example, QXL trades in London as well as on the Nasdaq Stock Market, meaning that its shares would likely be included in any general Nasdaq sell-off.

Mutual Fund Snapshot: Munder NetNet Fund

At a Glance
Established: 1996
Assets under management: $7.6 billion
2000 return: −56.75% (through Q3)
Return since inception: 37.26%
Fund managers: Steven Appledorn, Paul Cook, Alan Harris, Kenneth Smith, Brian Salerno

The oldest and largest of the Internet mutual funds, the Munder NetNet Fund is, for the moment, closed to new investors. But the Munder Funds group also includes an International NetNet Fund, which takes the same investment approach as its sister fund and applies it overseas, and a Future Technology Fund, which invests in emerging technology companies, though not necessarily those that are focused on the Internet.

Far more aggressive than many mutual funds, the NetNet Fund is nonetheless quite conservative by Internet fund standards. Though it invests in many pure-play Internet companies across subsectors, from B2B to B2C to infrastructure, the fund's prospectus is not so narrowly defined, allowing it to invest in companies the fund managers think stand to "benefit" from the Net, even if they are not Internet companies per se. Thus, at various times the Munder fund has invested in companies such as The Gap, which doesn't do the majority of its business on-line, but which Munder believes does enough business on-line that the company is the better for it. Still, the bulk of the fund is in companies that are highly related to the Internet—and has, at times, included large holdings of names such as VeriSign, InfoSpace, and Oracle.

This more balanced approach to the Internet sector means that NetNet Fund investors missed out on some of the biggest gains during the early days of the Internet euphoria. But it also means that they lost somewhat less than many other Internet fund holders did during the darkest days of the Internet sell-off of 2000. That said, the NetNet Fund is a targeted, sector-specific fund designed for investors with a stomach for risk.

Third, it's worth keeping in mind that many overseas stock markets aren't as developed as the U.S. markets are and lack the same degree of individual investor involvement. That means that foreign Internet stocks may not generate the same degree of enthusiasm among investors in their own countries as U.S. Internet stocks have generated among American investors. Translation? The stocks may not be awarded the same kinds of nosebleed valuations. That can be a good thing over the long term, because it means that these stocks may be relatively less expensive than their U.S. counterparts. But it may also mean that the stocks have less firepower in the short term.

An Index in Every Pot

Is there a way to avoid stock picking altogether—whether by you or by a fund manager—and simply buy into a basket of Net stocks to gain exposure to the sector? To some extent, there is. Just as various funds simply mimic the Standard & Poor's 500 index in a bid to represent the broad market, so, too, are funds beginning to spring up that track indexes of Internet stocks. Of course, indexes don't get around the human factor entirely. Like the S&P 500, the components of any stock index are selected by individuals, who may or may not pick winning stocks. The difference is that unlike actively managed mutual funds, index components tend not to change very often, frequently dropping out only after they merge, go out of business, or suffer from years of underperformance.

The benefit to indexing is that, over the very long run, this "passive" mimicking of the broad market has been shown to deliver returns comparable, if not superior, to "active" investing. In addition, index funds generally carry lower management fees than other mutual funds, where a fund manager's supposed stock-picking prowess comes at a premium.

The catch is twofold. First, while indexing to the broad market may make sense over the very long term, it's not at all clear that indexing to a particular sector offers the same kinds of benefits. Simply put, there are many fewer companies in the Internet sector than there are in the S&P 500, and most of them have much shorter track records. Given the sector's still emergent nature, the likelihood of some major development totally changing the business strategy and performance of a given Internet company is relatively high. The manager of an actively managed fund is paid to anticipate and cope with that kind of change. But stocks that are part of an index tend to stay there. That means the risk associated with Internet indexes may be higher than the risk associated with broader market indexes or even with indexes devoted to more mature market sectors. And while the management fees on a passively managed Internet fund may be lower than those on an actively managed fund, those savings can be counteracted in an instant if a fund's performance is lackluster.

Mutual Fund Snapshot: Monument Digital Technology Fund

At a Glance
Established: 1998
Assets under management: $79 million
2000 return: −56.88%
Return since inception: 100.88%
Fund manager: Bob Grandhi

Formerly known as the Monument Internet Fund, the renamed Digital Technology Fund was one of the first four Internet-focused mutual funds in the United States, as well as one of the first to alter that focus when Internet and technology stocks nose-dived in mid- to late 2000. The fund's management team argued that the shift reflected the view that "a narrow focus on dot coms is no longer justified as the Internet now reaches into virtually all aspects of the business world." Certainly, while that statement is increasingly true, it seems a noteworthy coincidence that the move came at a time when the fund was down 30 percent for the year to date.

Another noteworthy coincidence is that Monument sounds a lot like "momentum." Indeed, though its broader focus may suggest diminished risk, the Monument fund's momentum-driven approach remains high risk, though it arguably offers the potential for very high returns as well.

According to its managers, the fund seeks out companies that will "use the Internet to generate more profit and a higher stock price." As often as not, these will be bricks-and-mortar firms that use the Net to improve the efficiency of their supply chains or as a new distribution channel for their customers. In addition, the fund invests in hardware and software companies that stand to benefit from the broader integration of the Net into everyday life—companies such as Palm and Handspring, with their personal digital assistants, and even Sony, with its personal computers and PlayStation entertainment devices.

Second, there simply is no single, widely accepted index of Net stocks. Everybody and his kid brother, it seems, has developed an Internet index in the last few years, hoping to cash in on the enthusiasm for the sector as fund managers license the right to track those benchmarks. Companies offering Internet indexes include Dow Jones, publisher of *The Wall Street Journal*, CNET Networks, and TheStreet.com, as well as investment banks ranging from Goldman Sachs to Morgan Stanley. As it turns out, each of the various Internet indexes has a different approach. Some are weighted by the market capitalization of their component stocks. Others are weighted equally. Some include a broad selection of companies in a variety of different subsectors of the Internet economy, delving in some cases into companies only tangentially related to the Net. CNET's *Inter@ctive* Week @Net Index, for example, highlights fifty companies that are "key drivers of the development of the Internet." But the index's backers clearly have an expansive view of what it means to "drive the development of the Net." Among the index's components are 7-Eleven, the convenience store chain, which has an on-line presence but remains largely a bricks-and-mortar company. Other indexes feature a more focused selection. The Dow Jones Composite Internet Index, for example, includes only companies that derive at least 50 percent of their revenues from the Net.

As a result of these different approaches, the performance of the various indexes can vary widely. And while not every Internet index is yet linked to a tradeable security, the hope of each and every firm behind an index is that at some point its measure will become enough of an accepted benchmark that money managers will want to offer securities that track it.

One Fund or Several?

What does this all boil down to? It means that while investing in mutual funds can spare you the hassle and stress of picking individual stocks, investing in a single mutual fund may not solve the problem entirely. Certainly a well-run, broad-based fund can offer exposure to a variety of different Internet stocks. So, too, for an index fund. But depending on the fund's strategy—and the index's components—that approach may actually be more conservative—or more aggressive—than you, the investor, desire.

A supplement to—or substitute for—a broad Internet fund is a subsector-specific fund. Investors wishing to beef up their holdings in a particular category of Internet stock can use these types of funds to gain that kind of exposure. But such a strategy should be pursued with caution. Investing in one subsector to the exclusion of others puts you in double jeopardy, with the risk of a downturn in that category as well as the opportunity cost of missing out on any boom in other categories. A better approach is to use subsector funds to bolster one category among a broader portfolio of Internet stocks, or to use a medley of Internet funds to achieve the same kind of portfolio approach.

CHAPTER NINE

To Dot Com and Beyond

Life in the Post-PC World

I F WE TRIED to pinpoint the exact date on which the stock market's insane love affair with all things Internet ended, it would probably be April 14, 2000. Though the Nasdaq had actually peaked about one month earlier, it was on that day that fears the Federal Reserve would continue to raise interest rates, combined with a nagging concern that the mania over tech stocks had gone on for too long, precipitated a massive sell-off among tech stocks generally and Internet stocks specifically. Hardest hit at first were the consumer-oriented companies—portals, community sites, and e-commerce firms—with the weakest of them collapsing first. Shares of companies such as Beyond.com, Value America, theglobe.com, and Pets.com began falling victim to an accelerating and unrelenting erosion of value, losing billions of dollars in market capitalization as they ultimately plunged to stock prices in the low single digits. Over the next several months, some ended up filing for bankruptcy.

As confident as the market had once been that these companies would one day reverse their hemorrhaging of capital to become hugely profitable, it suddenly began to fear that that day would never come. And as the market's skittishness grew, it began to feed on itself, just as the euphoria had fed on itself earlier. Articles began predicting which dot coms would run out of cash first should they not be able to access the capital markets for a fresh round of financing. Venture capitalists, seeing the markets around them drying up, began pulling back their own dollars, refusing further funding for the most questionable businesses, orchestrating rapid-fire marriages of those they felt could no longer go it alone, and sometimes simply shutting companies down. A few sites saw the plug pulled by their backers before they even had an opportunity to launch.

As Wall Street analysts spoke of the "survival of the fittest," the sell-off spread beyond the consumer names to the business-to-business sector, the infrastructure sector, and the Internet incubators. Though the companies with the flimsiest business models succumbed first, eventually even the giants were dragged down with them. Compounding the problem was the fact that the summer tends to be a weak period for tech stocks as consumers and businesspeople alike go on vacation, leaving their computers behind. Internet usage drops, purchases sag, and trading volume on the stock market falls. This summertime slowdown led to relatively weak revenues for many companies in the Internet sector—a weakness that in days past would have been brushed off as nothing more than a seasonal lull but that in a time of general jitters fed fears that the headiest growth in on-line usage was past. As budgets were slashed to conserve cash, many dot coms scaled back their advertising spending, crimping the revenues of other, advertising-dependent dot coms in the process. From Amazon.com to eBay to Yahoo! in the consumer sector, from Commerce One to FreeMarkets in the business-to-business sector, from Inktomi to InfoSpace in the infrastructure sector, from CMGI to Internet Capital Group in the venture capital sector, all saw billions of dollars in market value erased beginning in the spring of 2000.

The Return to Normalcy

Some called the sell-off, and the ensuing wave of bankruptcies and mergers, a positive development, pointing out that it was eliminating the least viable players from the market and therefore making the competitive environment that much easier, over the long run, for the leaders. Others suggested it could only be a good thing for the market to return to something approaching a more rational valuation after the gravity-defying run-up in stock prices that had taken place in 1998, 1999, and early 2000. As much as companies had rushed to embrace the Internet when the mere mention of an Internet strategy—or the appendage of "dot com" to the end of a company's name—was enough to inflate a firm's value severalfold, so did they now rush to distance themselves from it. Some firms began dropping those "dot coms" from their names, trying to convince the market that they were more than "just" Internet companies.

Others went still further, abandoning or revamping strategies they had touted confidently just a short time earlier. By August, Amazon.com had struck its first far-reaching joint venture with a bricks-and-mortar retailer, Toys "R" Us—an alliance both companies would have considered anathema before the stock market compelled them to rethink their business models. Advertising-dependent companies such as Yahoo! and DoubleClick began breaking out the percentage of their clients that were stable *Fortune* 500 companies, as opposed to the now-questionable dot coms that had fueled their early growth. And CMGI, which had once boasted of its ability to invest in companies at pre-IPO values and then benefit enormously when they went public, announced a financial restructuring that would result in venture capital being relegated to just one of six revenue streams in the company's profit reports, part of an effort to convince investors that its fortunes weren't inextricably tied to the capital markets. The phrase "path to profitability"—a reference to the headlong dash by companies to reduce their cash burn and demonstrate the workability of their business models—became the favorite cliché of dot-com executives, analysts, and investors.

Without question, the market's wholesale abandonment of

many Internet companies was as extreme and unjustifiable as its earlier unfettered love for those companies had been. Unable or unwilling to see their potential flaws while the bubble was inflating, it suddenly seemed just as unable or unwilling to provide them with the time and support needed to prove their merits once the bubble had burst.

There is nevertheless much to be said for a more rational, skeptical, and slower-growing stock market. If it means that investment returns will, in the short term, pale in comparison to the spectacular levels achieved by some investors at the height of the dot-com euphoria, it also means that investors will have more realistic expectations not only of what the stock market can deliver, but also of what individual companies can hope to achieve in terms of revenues and profits and what pitfalls they may face. If it means that fewer young professionals will abandon careers in law, banking, and consulting to rush out to Silicon Valley and start their own Internet companies, it also means that entrepreneurs will be less tempted to start businesses simply for the sake of going public and striking the IPO jackpot. (A joke that circulated at Stanford Business School in the months after the April sell-off suggested that B2B and B2C stood for "Back to Banking" and "Back to Consulting.") And if it means that fewer firms have access to the capital markets or will achieve lower valuations when they get there, it also means that ill-prepared companies will be less inclined to rush full throttle into the market's arms, and will instead concentrate on proving that their business models can work.

Picking Up the Pace of Convergence

One consequence of forcing dot coms to focus more intently on the bottom line—and of causing investors to set more realistic growth expectations for their investments—is that the yawning chasm between virtual companies and traditional bricks-and-mortar companies has narrowed. Dot coms are still, by and large, growing far faster than their non-dot-com counterparts. But in many cases, as their businesses mature and they achieve greater scale, those spectacular growth rates are beginning to slow, from 100 percent and

200 percent year-over-year revenue jumps to still impressive, if less eye-popping, increases of 80 percent and even 50 percent. Potential market opportunities for many Internet businesses still appear far greater than those for their non-Internet rivals. But previous expectations of almost limitless markets now seem silly in retrospect. And though Internet executives occasionally still ridicule their old-economy rivals for "not getting it" about the Net or for being locked into old-fashioned ways of doing business, they are realizing, increasingly, that many old-economy companies have assets and expertise that are valuable and potentially useful. For example, in announcing its relationship with Toys "R" Us, Amazon.com highlighted not just Toys "R" Us's established brand—developed over decades as the country's leading toy retailer—but also its expertise in inventory management, a critical skill in the highly seasonal toy business and one that Amazon sorely lacked.

It doesn't take a fortune teller to figure out what these trends—the more rational valuations applied to dot coms in the market, the desire of some companies to dissociate themselves from the suggestion that they are purely virtual businesses, and the increasing linkages between old- and new-economy companies (whether through mergers of the AOL–Time Warner variety or joint ventures of the Amazon–Toys "R" Us type)—signify. Together, they herald the convergence of the on-line and off-line worlds—a time when the Internet has become a mechanism for doing business and a means of distributing goods and services, rather than the *only* way some companies do business or the *only* way they distribute goods. This isn't to suggest that the Net is any less important or revolutionary. To the contrary, it means that, as the Internet matures as a medium and as companies mature in their understanding of it, the Net will come to suffuse just about every aspect of every successful company. Companies that don't "get" the Net will still be relegated to the history books. Those that do "get" it will be more successful and more profitable than ever before. It will enhance their efficiency, increase their productivity, improve their sales, cut their costs, and do everything else, in spades, that it has only begun to do in its first decade as a commercial medium. But as that happens, the notion of "bricks-and-mortar" companies versus "Internet" companies, of a "new" economy versus an "old" economy, will fade from our vocabulary, since every company—even the most bricks-and-mortar intensive—will be an Internet company, and every company will be part of the new economy.

This might seem an odd way to conclude a book that has just spent some 200 pages laying out the various sectors and subsectors of the Internet economy. But those sectors and subsectors are as critically important to understand as ever. Companies in the future will still be divided among those that aim their products or services at consumers, those that aim them at other businesses, and those that build out the technological infrastructure of the Internet age. There will still be companies that invest in bringing other companies to market, and there will still be those that benefit more as bystanders to than direct participants in the technological revolution that is going on around them. The individual business models I've examined will evolve and converge. But the underlying principles emphasized—profitability, efficiency, adaptability, and solid management—will always differentiate companies that prosper from those that don't. In the same way, successful investing in the new, Internet-driven economy will be governed by the time-tested principles that have governed successful investing through the ages. Those are: knowing what you're putting your money behind, diversifying your portfolio so that it's not too heavily concentrated in any one area, investing with an eye toward the long term, and making investments that fit with your overall risk-return profile and at sensible valuations.

The Buck Rogers Era

But if the principles of successful investing remain unchanged, technology is continuing its forward march at an accelerating pace. Even as this book goes to press, new developments are rattling the Internet and media worlds, promising huge benefits for consumers and huge changes for businesses that have grown up amid older technologies. One of those is peer-to-peer computing, a technology that allows users to share files stored on one anothers' computer hard drives across corporate intranets or even across the Internet. To date, the most widely adopted form of this so-called P2P technology is the sharing of music files, with individuals around the world able to search each others' computers for particular songs and then download them to their own computers. While some forms of P2P technology rely on a central database to collect and distribute information on the location of those files, other variants don't require such centralization, making them extremely difficult to track or control. Consider the way this could change music distribution: rather than buying a compact disk from a retailer (whether on-line or off-line) or paying for the right to download music on-line (either directly from a label such as Warner Music or from a reseller like Amazon.com), users could simply share bootlegged copies of that music over the Net. So, too, for videos. The implications for the distribution of copyrighted material are huge. What's more, there are likely to be other applications of the technology that have yet to be discovered.

Wireless technology is another rapidly expanding frontier worth watching. Already, the distribution of cellular telephones and wireless personal digital assistants is exploding, and more and more of these devices are Web-enabled. It isn't hard to envision a day, quite soon, when many more people will be accessing the Internet through such handheld devices than through personal computers. The small screens and tiny keyboards that are part of most of these devices mean that traditional Web pages will need to be altered in some way to accommodate them. Most Internet companies are already working on developing wireless strategies, even as other companies are seeking to use the wireless Web in new ways, such as to direct mobile consumers to bricks-and-mortar stores that may be in their vicinity. Some companies will be more or less successful at making this transition from the desktop PC to the handheld device, meaning that new investment opportunities may materialize, even as other investments see their appeal diminished.

One technology still in its infancy that appears likely to work hand in hand with the wireless explosion is that of voice enabling. A host of companies are now experimenting with software and hardware that will understand and respond to spoken commands, allowing consumers to do away with keyboards entirely. Imagine being able to check and respond to your e-mail from your car without ever lifting your hands from the steering wheel. This day is nearly upon us, and the companies—many of them still privately held— that are able to develop the best technologies for this revolution might make intriguing investments.

Beyond these isolated examples of new technologies now being developed and perfected, there is the potential for many of these technologies to be combined and leveraged off of one another in new ways. Already, scientists are experimenting with Internet-ready clothes, home appliances, and even entire homes. Soon the day will come when working parents will be able to program their microwave ovens from their cellular phones while on the run—and have dinner waiting when they arrive. Once the stuff of Buck Rogers fantasies, these technologies are now within our reach.

What's more, there are countless other developments, as yet unimagined, that will change the way we live and the way we interact. Many will have the Internet at their core and are bound to become compelling investments. Others will fall by the wayside as quickly as many of the early, failed participants in the dot-com revolution. If there is one thing the early years of that revolution should have taught us, it's that in the world of technology investing there will always be hype and there will often be euphoria—but behind both there are bound to be at least a few great companies. No investor should expect to find all of them, and every investor should expect to make mistakes along the way. The successful investor will be the one who can find a few and then sit back and enjoy the ride.

Index